THE LORDS OF JAPAN

TREASURES OF THE WORLD

THE LORDS OF JAPAN

by

Henry Wiencek ·

Select
BOOKS

SELECT BOOKS
Treasures of the World was created and produced by Tree Communications, Inc., New York, N.Y.
First published in Great Britain 1983.

THE AUTHOR: Henry Wiencek is text editor on the staff of TREASURES OF THE WORLD at Tree Communications.

CONSULTANT FOR THIS BOOK: Robert D. Mowry, formerly assistant curator at the Fogg Art Museum at Harvard University, is curator of the Mr. and Mrs. John D. Rockefeller 3rd Collection of Asian Art at The Asia Society in New York.

ISBN 7054 1008 0

COVER: *Accompanied by the beat of drums and the wail of wind instruments, the official Japanese court dances, Bugaku, have enlivened imperial life since its beginnings. This dancer in a dragon mask is a detail from an early-eighteenth-century screen.*

TITLE PAGE: *A fully armored samurai on a magnificent mount rides to battle in this detail from a late-thirteenth-century scroll. He is one of the Minamoto clan, which eventually triumphed over its rivals and set up the first shogunate of Japan.*

OVERLEAF: *In this peaceful scene from a painted screen, young samurai frolic, and women dance. Watching from the platform at left are the mistress and son of Hideyoshi, the powerful regent who ruled all Japan in the late sixteenth century.*

ABOVE: *This angelic musician, carved of wood and seated upon a lotus beneath a floral canopy, is a treasure of seventh-century Nara, the first permanent capital. Buddhism flourished there, having come to Japan from the Asiatic mainland.*

CONTENTS

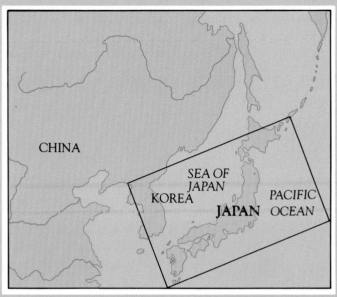

CHINA

SEA OF
JAPAN

KOREA

JAPAN

PACIFIC
OCEAN

S E A   O F   J A P A N

OKI
ARCHIPELAGO

TSUSHIMA

IKI

Danno-ura

ITSUKUSHIMA

Hiroshima

INLAND
SEA

SHIKOKU

KYUSHU

SATSUMA

Kanazawa

Himeji

Kyōto
(Imperial capital
794-1868)

Sekigahara

LAKE
BIWA

Bisai

Seto

Nagaoka
(Imperial capital 784-794)

Nagoya

Osaka

Nara
(Imperial capital
710-784)

Wakayama

Kōya

Ise

TANEGASHIMA

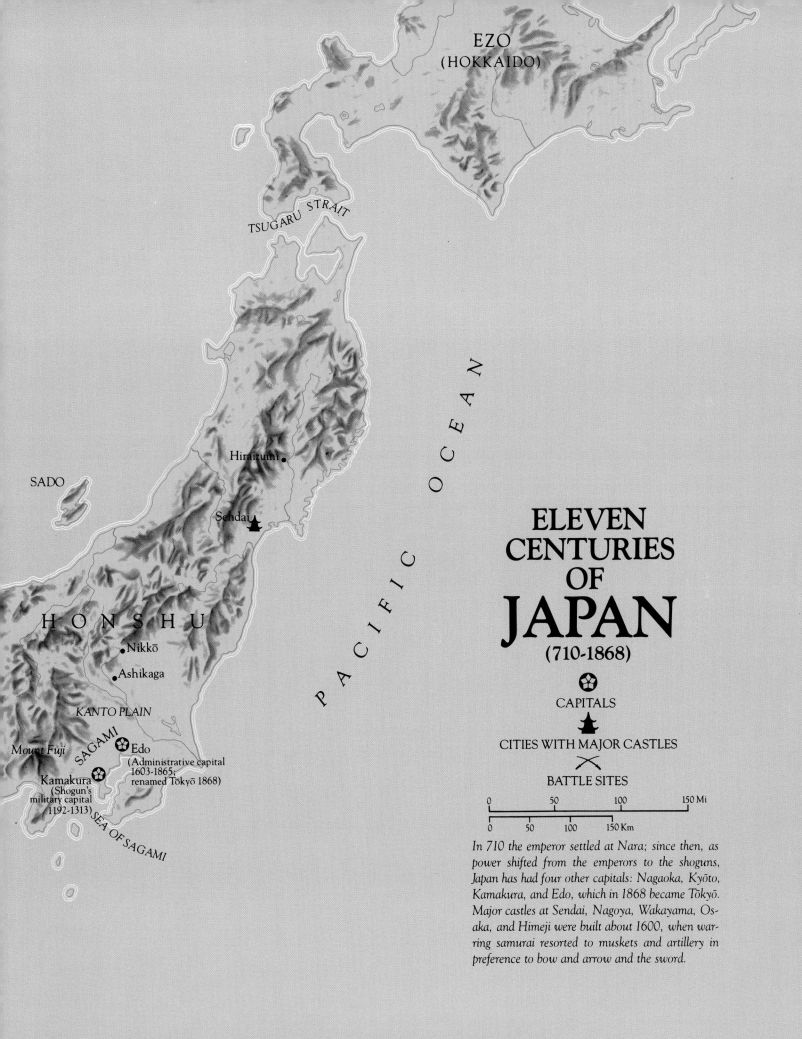

EZO
(HOKKAIDO)

TSUGARU STRAIT

PACIFIC OCEAN

SADO

Hiraizumi •

Sendai ▲

HONSHU

• Nikkō

• Ashikaga

KANTO PLAIN

Mount Fuji

SAGAMI ✿ Edo
(Administrative capital
1603-1865;
renamed Tōkyō 1868)

Kamakura ✿
(Shogun's
military capital
1192-1313)

SEA OF SAGAMI

ELEVEN CENTURIES OF JAPAN
(710-1868)

✿

CAPITALS

▲

CITIES WITH MAJOR CASTLES

✕

BATTLE SITES

| 0 | 50 | 100 | 150 Mi |

| 0 | 50 | 100 | 150 Km |

In 710 the emperor settled at Nara; since then, as power shifted from the emperors to the shoguns, Japan has had four other capitals: Nagaoka, Kyōto, Kamakura, and Edo, which in 1868 became Tōkyō. Major castles at Sendai, Nagoya, Wakayama, Os-aka, and Himeji were built about 1600, when war-ring samurai resorted to muskets and artillery in preference to bow and arrow and the sword.

I

THE FIRST EMPERORS

THE TREASURE HOUSE OF NARA

At the beginning of time a god and goddess stood on the heavenly floating bridge—a rainbow—and gazed at the earth below. Lowering the heavenly jeweled spear into the ocean, they stirred the waters, causing a churning sound; and when they lifted the spear, drops of water fell from its tip, became solid, and turned into an island. The two deities descended to the land, where the goddess gave birth to the Great Eight Island Country—Japan— and to the goddess of the sun, Amaterasu, who was to rule over the new country.

The sun goddess whose birth is described in this creation myth was the great-great-grandmother of another mythical figure, Emperor Jimmu, the legendary founder of the Japanese imperial family. All succeeding emperors were his descendants and thus the direct descendants of the sun goddess. Throughout Japanese history, even in times when imperial power was overshadowed by the might of wealthy families and warlords, the emperor has been looked on as the sacred chief, the symbol of Japan's unity and perpetuity. Each

Shōmu, here in gold, amassed one of the first great collections of treasures in Japan. This portrait of the eighth-century emperor and his priests is from a hanging scroll.

The Buddha sits, serenely and safely, in a flaming pavilion, proving to skeptics that he is indeed the "enlightened one." According to the eighth-century scroll from which this detail comes, the Buddha's miracle of the inferno won new converts.

emperor has possessed three treasures, reputedly handed down to Jimmu from heaven, that are the signs of the divine origin of the emperor—the mirror of the sun goddess, signifying the emperor's divinity; a sword, representing his power; and a jewel, taken from the steps of heaven, representing wisdom.

According to the legend of Jimmu, he took possession of the Yamato region, near the future capital of Kyōto, after battling against a barbarian people. The barbarians were probably the Ainu, a white-skinned race of hunters and fishermen who might have come from eastern Siberia to Japan about 3000 B.C. The legend of Jimmu probably reflects actual fighting between the Ainu and the ancestors of the Japanese—a variety of peoples that came to Japan from southern China, Indochina, and perhaps from islands in the Pacific. Some of them were farmers who brought methods of raising rice, a crop that became the mainstay of the Japanese diet.

The early Japanese believed that the land was thronged with *kami*, or "spirits," some good, some evil. The spirits could be heard speaking from the rocks, trees, mountains, lakes, and fields they inhabited. From this belief in spirits evolved the national Japanese cult, called Shintō, "The Way of the Spirits." Its precepts are vague; but the basic belief is that virtually everything in nature possesses a spirit and is alive in some way. The Japanese venerated the spirits by chanting the names of the kami and sought divine aid in farming or warfare with offerings of food or models of animals and weapons.

Shintō had no moral code and no concept of sin; but it did have a complex code of laws regarding purity. Bloodshed, for example, defiled a person, so a woman who had given birth and a man wounded in battle were considered impure. They could cleanse themselves by ritual washing. However, a house where an emperor died could not be purified and had to be abandoned.

The emperor acted as the overseer of the national purity. In the Great Purification Liturgy he asked the gods to cleanse the land of such polluting offenses as killing, performing witchcraft, planting weeds, or damaging irrigation works. The fertility of Japan's fields was another of the emperor's official concerns. Every spring he offered the prayer for harvest, addressing the gods of harvest, growth, wells, gateways, islands, farms, uplands, and streams.

The deeds of Japan's early emperors and the events of their reigns were chronicled in the seventh century A.D. The annals tell of frequent wars between clans over land, which was the only source of wealth. There were few gold and silver mines, and the primitive mining techniques of the era recovered just a fraction of these lodes. Families tough enough to stake out and hold large farms became the nobility of early Japan. About A.D. 300 a confederation of clans recognized an emperor, whose seat was in the Yamato region, but relinquished to him almost none of their independence. Clan chiefs continued to reign over their land and the peasants who farmed for them. The landowners provided their peasants with protection from rival clans, but little else. Despite occasional reforms, the lot of the Japanese peasant has been a meager one. The landowner took most of the harvest, and the portion left to the farmer was often heavily taxed by the emperor.

Since farming was the heart of the economy, rice and seeds were the national currencies, and even farm tools could be used as money. Until the first century A.D., Japanese farmers used implements of bronze, a relatively soft and easily broken material. Seafaring clans from western Kyūshū visited Korea in the first century and found the farmers there using much sturdier tools of iron, made in China. Kyūshū traders imported these tools, and from this small beginning grew a lively trade among Japan, Korea, and China. Farm tools were followed by gold and silver ornaments, precious silks and brocades, and paintings and books that awed the Japanese. Chinese and Korean artists found eager patrons among Japan's upper class.

Far from being too proud to admit the superiority of China, the Japanese embraced Chinese culture and sought to learn all they could from their highly sophisticated neighbor. The Japanese, who had developed only a primitive form of writing, painstakingly studied Chinese script and adapted it to the Japanese language. Scholars traveled to China to scrutinize the methods of government, with the result that the Japanese installed a Chinese-style bureaucracy in their

Mononobe Moriya, a sixth-century chieftain who resisted the introduction of Buddhism, calls from his horse for the destruction of a Buddhist temple, as the devout run for their lives. This scene is from a five-paneled painting on silk made in 1069.

IN HIS OWN IMAGE

Prince Shōtoku, regent to Empress Suiko, built a complex of temples called the Hōryū-ji early in the seventh century to enshrine some of the first masterpieces of Japanese Buddhist art. The magnificent Buddha and two bodhisattvas—benevolent deities—at left came to the Hōryū-ji when Suiko and others commissioned Tori Busshi, the first great sculptor in Japan, to create the trinity as an offering for the prince, who was ailing. The gilded bronze sculpture is as much a monument to the prince as to his god.

The Buddha, sitting in the lotus position of meditation and allegedly scaled to Shōtoku's size, wears a humble monk's robe, reminding his followers of his renunciation of the world. The *urna*, the dot representing a third eye, in the center of his forehead sees all; his large ears hear all; and the *ushnisha*, the raised knot on top of his head, indicates that he possesses all knowledge. The position of the Buddha's right hand means that the faithful need have no fear, while his left index and middle fingers extend in charity.

The standing bodhisattvas—their smaller stature appropriate to their rank beneath the Buddha—are dressed as Indian princes. Each holds a jewel, symbolizing the spiritual riches due the devout.

Clouded with incense, the sacred sculpture dominated great occasions in the Golden Hall of the Hōryū-ji. The prince never recovered from his illness, and in 622 he died. The golden triad became a votive offering for Shōtoku's rebirth in paradise.

His own great dignity and serenity shared by his haloed saints, Shakyamuni—the historical Buddha—reflects the inner harmony and peace that was sought by his followers.

own country. The Japanese capacity for absorbing a foreign culture was prodigious, but so was their genius for assimilating something exotic, adapting it, and making it their own. From the books, paintings, and beautiful treasures of China, Japan gradually created a distinctly Japanese culture.

To a large degree Chinese influence on Japan was filtered through nearby Korea, and it was from Korea that Japan received a gift, in the sixth century, that was to have the most profound impact on Japanese life. The ruler of the Korean kingdom of Paekche, beset by warlike neighbors, had been sending presents regularly to Japan in the hope of getting ships to fend off his enemies. In 552 he dispatched ambassadors to Japan with the most valuable gift he could find, accompanied by an extravagant message: "Imagine a man in possession of treasures to his heart's content, so that he might satisfy all his wishes.... Thus it is with the treasure of this wonderful doctrine." The gift he had sent was Buddhism. The Paekche ambassadors carried to Japan books of Buddhist doctrine and a gold and copper image of the Buddha.

When Buddhism came to Japan it was already a very old doctrine, based on the life of a sixth-century-B.C. Indian named Gautama, later called the Buddha, or the "enlightened one." Appalled by the misery of life in India and the inevitability of sickness and death, Gautama sought an explanation through fasting and meditation. He failed at first, but while sitting beneath a tree he received enlightenment. Gautama came to believe that there was no god, no soul, and that the world is only an illusion. He spread his enlightenment through preaching, but did not write down his teachings. After the Buddha's death, his followers recorded a series of dialogues called sutras, containing their master's teachings. Buddhist philosophy holds that to exist is to suffer, but that one may seek release from suffering through the so-called eightfold path of right views, right resolve, right speech, right action, right livelihood, right effort, right mindedness, and right concentration.

Buddhism was firmly established in Japan just a few decades after its introduction by the famous Prince Shōtoku, the greatest scholar

Two men play lutes—one of the instruments smaller than the other and played with a bow—as their companions listen and take refreshment from a server. This blissful scene is from the leather-and-sandalwood surface of an eighth-century lute.

in Japan, who ruled as regent from 593 to 622 on behalf of his aunt, the empress. Shōtoku encouraged the founding of Buddhist monasteries and the conversion of the people to Buddhism. Aside from his energetic support of the new doctrine, Shōtoku also wrote a set of moral maxims to guide the actions of the government and the people, tried to shift the balance of power from clan leaders to the throne, and spurred on the nation to emulate the culture of China, which the prince admired deeply.

Shōtoku's benevolent and widely popular reign ended with his death in 622, a death that signaled the start of decades of intrigue, culminating in a bloody coup. Soga Emishi, the head of the Soga family and great minister under Shōtoku, contrived to have Shōtoku's oldest son, Yamishiro Oe, passed over for the succession and installed his own candidate on the throne. Emishi then placed the real power of the government in the hands of his son Iruka.

The usurpations of Soga Emishi paled next to the naked ambition of Iruka. Fearing that Shōtoku's son might assert a claim to the throne, Iruka decided to kill him. Yamashiro Oe knew that resistance to Iruka would spark a civil war and sent a message to his supporters saying, "Is it only when one has conquered in battle that he is to be called a hero? Is he not also a hero who has made safe his country at the expense of his own life?" Then the prince and his entire family committed suicide.

The prince's supporters obeyed his last wish and kept their peace; but a nobleman named Nakatomi Kamatari resolved to check the rising power of the Soga. Kamatari enlisted the aid of a prince, and the two conspirators laid their plans in a series of conversations—ostensibly devoted to discussions of Chinese philosophy—in a wisteria garden. At a solemn court ceremony, the prince, Kamatari, and two hired swordsmen assassinated Iruka; on the following day Soga Emishi was executed.

The assassination not only toppled the Soga family, it brought another family into Japanese history—the clan of the conspirator Kamatari. They received a new name to commemorate the wisteria garden where Kamatari and the prince had plotted. The Japanese word for wisteria is *fuji*, and the new family—one destined to rule Japan for two centuries—was named the Fujiwara.

Kamatari and the prince decreed a number of reforms in 646. Chief among them was land reform: they took farmland away from the country clans and gave it to the peasants, hoping to break the power of the clans. In fact the reform did little to help the peasants or to bring down the landowners. Unable to pay the expenses of farming and the burdensome taxes, the peasants mortgaged their new land to the wealthy clans and to tax-exempt Buddhist monasteries and ended up as poor as ever.

One of the provisions of the reforms of 646 was that the capital of the emperor be established in one place. Previously the court moved after the death of an emperor because of the Shintō belief that death polluted a place. Thus the emperors usually resided in crude houses, not far removed from log cabins. But having heard travelers' descriptions of the majestic cities of China, Japanese courtiers yearned to have something as magnificent. They selected a site for the capital in a valley at Nara, where court architects laid out a grid pattern covering thirty-five square miles.

One of the first Nara emperors was Shōmu, who ascended the throne in 724. The emperor whose recent predecessors had lived in cabins found himself the resident of a splendid building with a tiled roof in the center of a city. In this palace Shōmu padded about the felt-covered floors in scarlet leather shoes with turned-up toes, adorned with gold and silver flowers studded with pearls. He wore a belt of moleskin over his brocade blouse, and he amused himself with archery, rowing, riding, and falconry, leaving the affairs of state to the Fujiwara.

Shōmu, his family, and his courtiers were deeply devoted to Buddhism. Because the taking of life was sinful in Buddhist belief, Shōmu's daughter the empress Kōken for a short time forbade the killing of any animals in Japan and paid fishermen out of the imperial treasury to make up for their lost livelihood. The piety of Shōmu's wife, Kōmyō, inspired the legend that she washed a thousand beggars to demonstrate her humility. The last beggar was a leper, and

Robed gentlemen, gathered beneath pine trees, play go—a board game popular among the leisure class first in ancient China, then in Japan. The pitcher in front of the board might hold wine. An unknown eighth-century artist painted this scene on a leather medallion decoration on a lute.

Kichijō-ten, in the eighth-century portrait above, occupied an important position in the Japanese Buddhist pantheon: she not only forgave sins but could reward devotees. Here, in embroidered robes, diaphanous veils, and jewelry (she holds a jewel in her left hand), Kichijō-ten looks less the ethereal goddess than an elegant lady of the court.

when the empress, without hesitation, washed his body, he ascended into the sky—a sign of the Buddha's approval of her good works.

When a plague of smallpox broke out in the countryside, Shōmu sought divine aid to rescue Japan from the scourge. He resolved to found a Buddhist monastery, the Tōdai-ji, where he planned to erect a gigantic statue of the Buddha Vairocana—the cosmic Buddha who rules over a myriad of realms and lesser Buddhas. Shōmu asked the help of the whole country to complete the project. He solicited money from the rich and exhorted each peasant to bring "a bundle of grass" for the furnace or "a handful of soil" for the statue's clay mold. He ordered every bronze object in the realm to be melted down for the statue. The statue was built in forty-one stages to a height of fifty-three feet—a job that took two years. Another year and a half was needed just to cast the 966 curls on the statue's head. The most difficult task—carving decorations for the statue and gilding it—required two decades and exhausted Japan's gold supply. But as the statue was being gilded, a new gold mine was discovered—a timely find hailed as a miracle. All told, the statue used up about a million pounds of copper, tin, and lead and five hundred pounds of gold.

On April 9, 752, Shōmu marched in solemn procession to the temple of the Great Buddha, where ten thousand priests awaited the ceremony of dedication. Inside the temple crimson fabrics covered the floor, and candlelight illumined clouds of incense rising about the statue. Shōmu slowly climbed up a scaffold to the face of the Buddha high above the floor. He took up a brush, which was attached to a silk cord long enough for thousands of spectators to take hold of it and symbolically join with Shōmu as he gravely painted the black eyes of the Buddha.

When Shōmu died in 756, Kōmyō moved his possessions to a building called the Shōsō-in on the grounds of the Great Buddha's temple. For twelve centuries Japan's emperors have personally supervised the Shōsō-in—its doors must be sealed with a paper bearing the reigning emperor's signature and are opened only once every year—and guarded Shōmu's paintings, musical instruments, clothing, and furniture as national treasures.

THE SEALED TREASURY

In 757, a year after Emperor Shōmu's death, mourners carried this gilt-bronze chintaku, *or pacifying bell, which hung from a banner at the memorial service.*

Emperor Shōmu founded the Tōdai-ji, an immense temple complex at Nara, and, with his empress Kōmyō, attended great ceremonies there. Aristocrats in eighth-century Japan vied for invitations to the palace of the royal couple, and the hunts, banquets, dances, dramas, and religious ceremonies were invariably elegant affairs and glorious spectacles.

Shōmu amassed thousands of things to beautify his palace and temples, patronizing Japanese craftsmen and the traders who brought exotic goods from Persia, India, and China. A devout Buddhist, Shōmu commissioned religious art; gilded images of deities were dear to him. When Shōmu died in 756, his widow gathered the things that had made the emperor happiest—musical instruments, ceramics, lacquered furniture—and gave them to the Tōdai-ji, where they were placed in the Shōsō-in storehouse.

Here and on the following pages is a selection from the Shōsō-in: a lute as beautiful to see as to hear, an exquisite eight-sided box, an intricately lacquered incense burner. The contents of Shōmu's storehouse attest to the splendid ceremonies at the Tōdai-ji and the glory of Nara.

Musical instruments provided one of life's pleasures at the Imperial Palace at Nara. The lute at left, of chestnut and red sandalwood, may have come to Emperor Shōmu from China in the eighth century. In the detail opposite, the mother-of-pearl and tortoiseshell inlay sets the instrument in the faraway tropics: a musician on camelback strums his lute beneath a banana tree.

The banjolike genkan, one of Emperor Shōmu's favorite musical instruments, enlivened state occasions at the Imperial Palace. Mother-of-pearl inlays in myriad patterns decorate this red sandalwood genkan, both sides of which are shown. On the back of the instrument, below, two parrots—exotic birds to the Japanese—hold jeweled streamers in their beaks, indicating high rank.

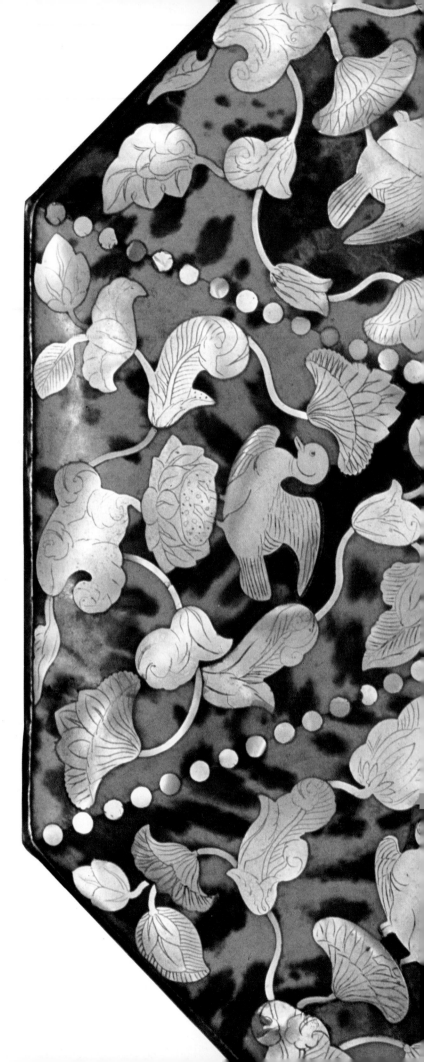

Vines, flowers, and birds—in mother-of-pearl and tortoiseshell—cover the octagonal box above and in detail at right, which a craftsman made from the wood of a mulberry tree. Emperor Shōmu might have stored a polished bronze hand mirror in the box, keeping it in his bedchamber at his palace. The Japanese believed that mirrors reflected the purity of one's soul.

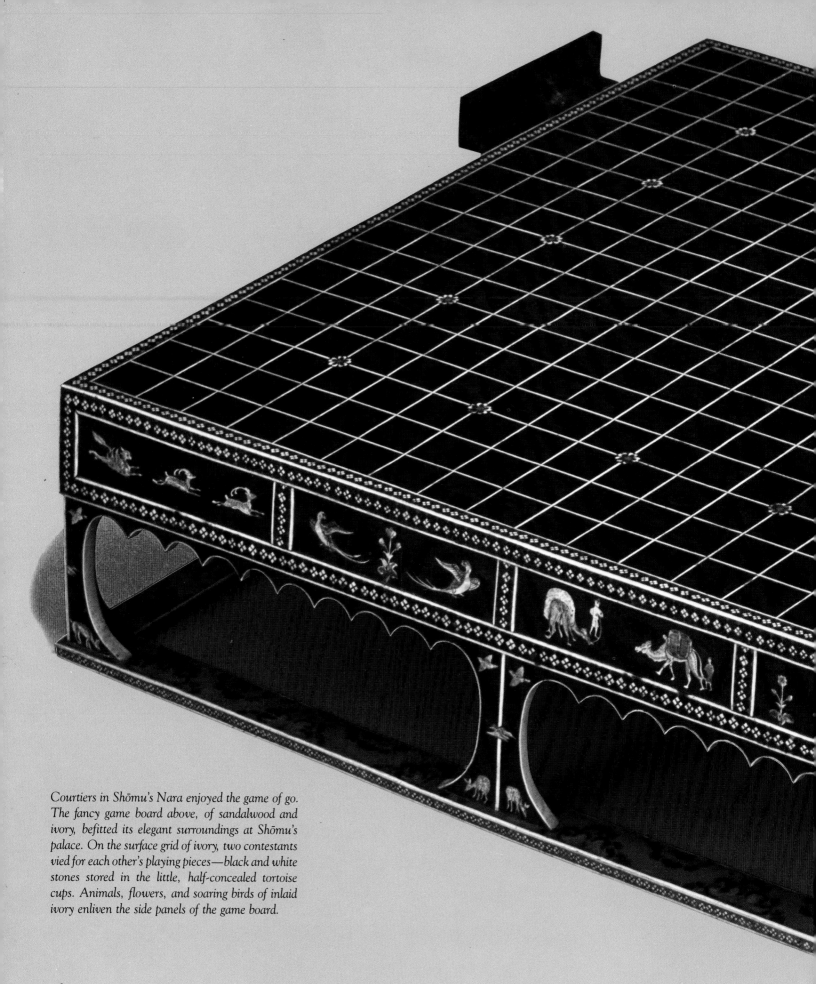

Courtiers in Shōmu's Nara enjoyed the game of go. The fancy game board above, of sandalwood and ivory, befitted its elegant surroundings at Shōmu's palace. On the surface grid of ivory, two contestants vied for each other's playing pieces—black and white stones stored in the little, half-concealed tortoise cups. Animals, flowers, and soaring birds of inlaid ivory enliven the side panels of the game board.

28

Perfumes smoldered at Tōdai-ji religious ceremonies in beautiful censers such as the long-handled burner below and in detail at left. A lion, a lotus blossom of gilded copper, and crystal-eyed flowers decorate the censer of red sandalwood, which may have held incense at Shōmu's funeral.

A lotus blossom—over twenty inches across—
blooms from the base of a bronze censer that burned
incense as an offering to the Buddha. Gold leaf trims
each of the thirty-two lacquered, multicolored petals
that are clustered around the bowl. Lions, birds, and
flowers decorate the petals of the lotus, which itself
represents the earth.

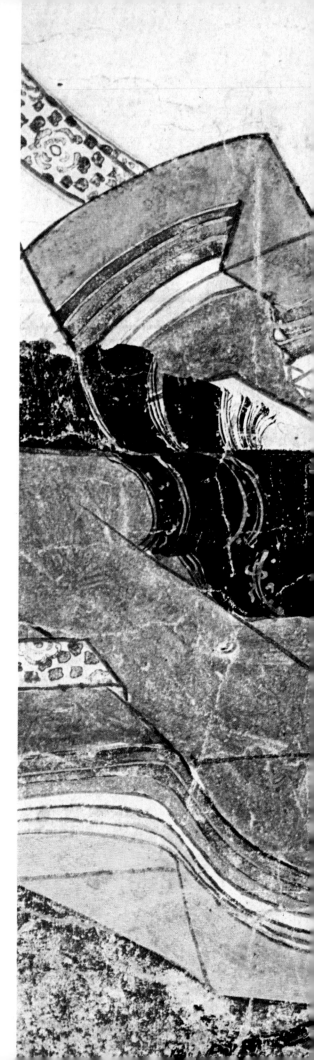

II

ROYAL LADIES OF KYOTO

EXQUISITE LIVES IN THE HEIAN AGE

Early one morning, when a pale moon still hung in the sky, we went out into the garden, which was thick with mist. . . . Her Majesty got up herself, and all the ladies in attendance joined us in the garden. As we strolled about happily, dawn gradually appeared on the horizon. . . .'So you have been out moon-viewing,' said [a gentleman] admiringly and composed a poem in praise of the moon."

Thus does Sei Shōnagon, a tenth-century lady-in-waiting to the empress Sadako, describe a pre-dawn "moon-viewing" in her memoir, *The Pillow Book*, a collection of vignettes of court life. The incident recounted by Sei Shōnagon reveals a great deal about aristocratic court society—about its highly refined tastes, its love for nature, and its romantic search for beauty. The pale setting moon, shining down on a garden shrouded in a mist soon to be burned away by the sun, created a scene of delicate, fleeting beauty, which the courtiers cherished intensely because it was so evanescent.

This scene took place in Heian-kyō, the capital built in the late eighth and early ninth century and later named Kyōto. In 784 the

In her portrait from a biographical scroll, the poet Ko-ō-gimi sports the shaved, painted eyebrows and mane of hair favored by stylish beauties.

This painting of a bark-shingled house beneath a red maple tree commemorates a poetry contest in which the poets described the landscapes of a chosen region. The writer settling to her work inside warms herself by a small fire, for it is autumn, the most melancholy season.

emperor Kammu had decided to move the capital from Nara to Nagaoka to escape the political interference of the Buddhist temples in Nara. But ten years later, for the site of a new capital, the emperor chose a lovely valley where his surveyors and architects laid out a rectangular city, three and one-half miles long and three miles wide, crisscrossed by eighteen avenues. Heian-kyō, which means "capital of peace and tranquillity," gave its name to the Heian period—a time when Kyōto was home to a glamorous society, dominated by the Fujiwara family.

Kyōto society was devoted to the pleasures of love and art. For the city's aesthetes, artists devised uniquely Japanese styles in sculpture, painting, and the decorative arts. Painters, for example, gave increasing attention to Japanese life, rather than to religious themes derived from Chinese Buddhist art. They painted scenes of wealthy households from a bird's-eye perspective, so that the viewer seemed to be peeking down into the rooms of a house from which the roof had been removed.

In the decorative arts the most popular medium was lacquer, a clear varnish that artists applied to cosmetics boxes, bottles, tables, and even saddles. Sometimes the artist inlaid these pieces with mother-of-pearl, or sprinkled gold or silver dust onto a piece before coating it, so that the precious powder glittered through the lacquer in a splendid interplay of colors.

The courtiers had a special appreciation for subtle combinations of colors, particularly in clothing. Both men and women donned layer upon layer of silk, each layer of a different hue. As women were driven through the streets of the city in their closed, ox-drawn carriages, they exposed their sleeves through the window—a coy display that was considered highly erotic. In *The Pillow Book*, Sei Shōnagon links romance to the attractiveness of a man's clothes. "Charming. . . is the sight of a young man clad in laced trousers of dark purple and in a dazzling Court robe over an array of varicolored garments, as he leans forward into the woman's room, pushing aside the green blind."

In this sophisticated circle, everyone was a poet. Lovers corresponded in verse, officials sought favors by writing poems, and any event, no matter how trivial, was instantly recorded in a few lines of poetry and passed among the courtiers. In this literary atmosphere, where a few wisps of ink on colored paper were a treasure and where the courtiers were the subjects of their own daily outpouring of verse, the boundary between life and art was transparent, if it existed at all.

The two most prominent writers of the Heian period were women—Sei Shōnagon and Murasaki Shikibu, who were the leaders in establishing a native Japanese literature. Whereas men continued to write in Chinese, women wrote in Japanese prose and fashioned a vivid literary language unfettered by archaic Chinese genres. Lady Murasaki is famous for writing one of the world's first and greatest novels, the *Tale of Genji*, in which she chronicled the loves and intrigues of Kyōto society. Lady Murasaki may have based her chief character, Genji, on the regent Michinaga—a member of the Fujiwara family, which ruled Kyōto from behind the throne and set its own special stamp on that dazzling time.

The foundation of the Fujiwara family's power at court was its great and ever-expanding wealth. Farmland remained the source of money in Japan, and the Fujiwara held vast tracts of it. The family received much of its land from various emperors in payment for services. Not only did the throne gradually lose territory through these gifts, it lost additional revenues because the grants were tax-exempt. As the Fujiwara grew in wealth, the emperors became impoverished and dependent on the Fujiwara to pay the expenses of the court.

The Fujiwara used their power not for any political end, but only for their own continued enrichment. They embarked on no great military campaigns, nor did they attempt to set up any system for national rule. In fact the whole Kyōto court held itself aloof from the rest of the country. Courtiers embraced the Chinese notion that the chief duty of the emperor and his highest aides was to enact court rituals with the utmost punctilio. When officials from the provinces arrived at court to present reports about the harvest, the emperor's ministers concerned themselves only with the appearance of the documents—whether the seals were affixed in accordance with

On a moonlit night a Fujiwara nobleman pays an impromptu visit to the quarters of the ladies-in-waiting at the Imperial Palace. Lady Murasaki, the great novelist of the Heian court, wrote in her diary that, though the nobleman and a companion sang and teased, the ladies held their door closed.

custom, whether signatures were written in the correct places—and with the way officials spoke and dressed. The abundance of the harvest—or lack of it—was a trifling matter to be left to subordinates.

Court documents were written in a rarified version of Chinese, comprehensible only to a tiny handful of cognoscenti. A dispute over the wording of one such document brought Kyōto to the brink of chaos in the ninth century. The emperor Uda, wishing to delegate authority to Fujiwara Mototsune, requested his court scholar to draw up the appropriate papers. The scholar did so, using in one passage the archaic Chinese word *ako*, meaning literally "reliance on equity." The choice of ako was intended merely to add a literary flourish to the text, much as if a modern speechwriter were to quote Shakespeare. But the scholars in the employ of Mototsune interpreted ako strictly and took it to imply that the emperor was not imparting executive authority to Mototsune but merely moral authority, based on a notion of equity. To demonstrate that the city needed a vigorous, active minister, Mototsune released a herd of wild horses into the streets as a challenge to the emperor's power to keep order. The emperor's response was to summon a conclave of scholars to elucidate the nuances of ako—a task that required several months of study and debate. Meanwhile, as the discussion took place, the city slipped into anarchy.

Disorder in the capital was nothing new to its inhabitants, for it was an open secret that the emperor had virtually no military power. Though a royal guard force nominally protected the emperor and the capital, these guards were little more than armed idlers, more dangerous than the brigands they were supposed to keep in check. The guards galloped through the streets of the city, threatening citizens and taking what they wished. On one occasion the guards blockaded the city gates because they hadn't been paid. With no effective police force to stop them, thieves ran riot in Kyōto, even entering the palace itself, looting, killing, destroying, and burning with impunity.

The emperors made matters worse with their Buddhist aversion to physical punishment and with their sublime ignorance of the real-

THE TYRANNY OF MANNERS

Twelfth-century gentlewomen enjoyed great sexual and intellectual liberty and rivaled men in the characteristic pastimes of the period: contests of aesthetic connoisseurship and romantic and political intrigues. Well-reared women were educated in the arts. They contributed to the development of the first practical Japanese syllabary, or set of letters, and, especially in their poems, the first uniquely Japanese literary voice. At the same time the Kyōto court's elaborate etiquette and preoccupation with style formalized the behavior of both sexes. Women were cloistered, and their personal artfulness was equaled by the artificialities of custom.

For a lady to be seen standing upright was indelicate, and gentlefolk looked with horror upon the naked human body, white female teeth, and less-than-white skin. Her teeth blackened and face heavily powdered, the lady dressed for society in twelve different-colored kimonos. The layered colors showing at wrist, neck, and hem expressed her artistry and wit, and sometimes her rank. Men had a difficult time catching a glimpse of a lady's face, for even in sleep she covered it with a cloth. But the edges of her huge garments trailing out of her carriage window or beneath a screen inflamed her suitor's hopes. If she grew unhappy in love, she would write him a poem saying that her sleeves, rather than her cheeks, were "wet with tears."

The poet Saigū Nyōgo reclines on a mat, engulfed by her own kimonos, her writing box nearby. The curtain shields her from idle male glances, but has openings to slip hands and objects through.

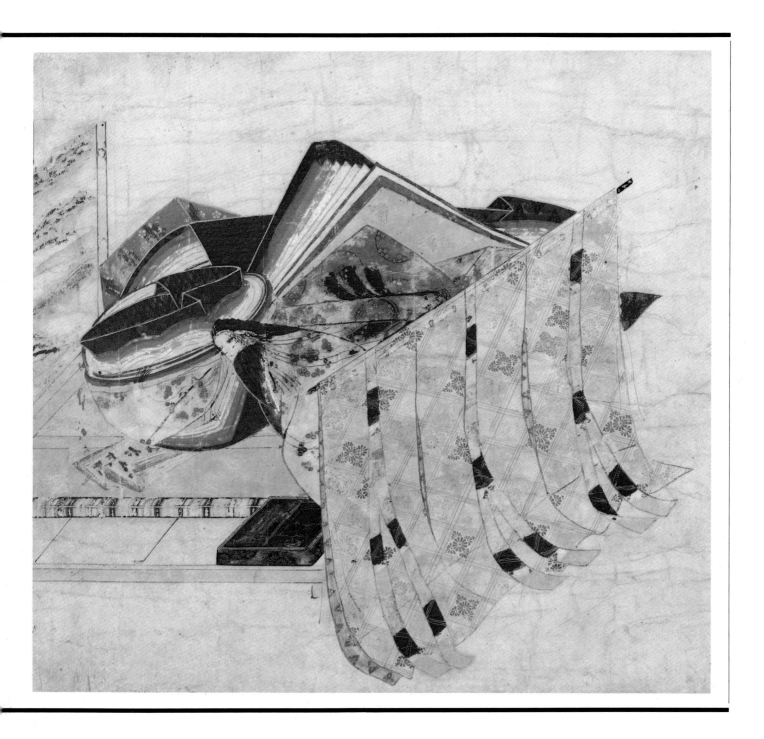

ities of city life. One emperor, touring the poor wards, came upon a building crowded with men and asked whose residence this strange place was. When told it was a prison, the emperor set all the inmates free and was cheered by the mob of convicts with cries of "banzai," a cheer of triumph.

In the countryside the situation was equally chaotic. The roads from the capital into the country were little more than trails scratched out of mountainsides. A journey of a few hundred miles took months, so even if the emperor wished to keep a firm hand on events in outlying regions, he could not. In any case the emperor and his court preferred to let country barons take care of any trouble. On one occasion, when reports of an uprising in the provinces reached the capital, the court delayed sending a relief force for forty days, because they were waiting for the most auspicious day to travel. When Korean pirates besieged towns along the western coast, the court managed to avoid paying any reward to the victorious defenders on the pretext that the battle had ended before the arrival of official orders.

The indifference of the emperors to affairs outside the capital created a vacuum that allowed the country families to rule their regions independently and with increasing vigor and wealth. This development did not go unnoticed by the Fujiwara: it was a family talent to turn apparent weaknesses into strengths. Late in the tenth century, Fujiwara Michinaga realized that the newfound might of the country barons, properly applied by the right man, could end the disarray in the city. But first Michinaga had to contend with a rival in his own family.

In his rise to power Michinaga showed adroitness—typical of his family—at finding a way for romance to advance his cause. Michinaga's rival for the regency, Fujiwara Korechika, was having an affair with a woman who shared living quarters with the lover of a retired emperor, Kazan. (Kazan had already experienced the guile of the Fujiwara. He had been tricked into becoming a monk when a Fujiwara persuaded the emperor to join him in entering a monastery. As they were approaching the monastery, the Fujiwara said he

Michinaga, the supreme Fujiwara statesman, watches approvingly as luxurious Chinese-style barges with phoenix and dragon figureheads glide across his ornamental pond. He had the barges built in honor of Emperor Ichijō, who was coming to call.

wanted to pay one last visit to his family. Kazan entered the priesthood; the Fujiwara never returned.) Michinaga spread the rumor that Kazan was visiting Korechika's lover. Korechika decided to find out for himself and hid in his lover's garden one night. When Kazan appeared the jealous Korechika fired an arrow, grazing the ex-emperor's sleeve—an offense serious enough to get him banished, leaving Michinaga a clear path.

Michinaga ruled from behind the thrones of five emperors, from 995 to 1028, bringing the fortunes of the Fujiwara family to their height. He put a stop to the disorder in the city by allying himself with the Minamoto, a family of tough fighting men from the countryside. Minamoto warriors, known as the "nails and teeth" of Michinaga, imposed order on Kyōto and, of course, made any attempt by the emperors to oust Michinaga by force impossible.

In the Fujiwara tradition Michinaga consolidated his hold on the throne through marriage. He was lucky enough to be the father of four daughters. He installed one of them in a magnificent house, and she became, at the age of twelve, a consort of the emperor Ichijō. Ichijō fretted under the domination of Michinaga, abdicated at the age of thirty-one in 1011, and died shortly thereafter, worn down by the intrigues of the Fujiwara. The next emperor, Sanjō, also found himself saddled with one of Michinaga's daughters as a wife. But Michinaga's marriage policy reached its extreme with the following two emperors: their Fujiwara wives were their own aunts.

Under Michinaga society glittered as never before in its splendid city. Poets called Kyōto the "city of purple hills and crystal streams," after the hills that protected the city on three sides and the two rivers that flowed past the eastern and western walls. The crystal streams ran through the heart of the city in canals down the centers of the boulevards. The water reflected the willow trees along the curbs— trees that glowed like delicate green jewels when they caught the sunlight, in the image of one Kyōto poet.

Lining the main boulevards were the mansions of the rich. A wealthy family's grounds typically covered three and one-half acres and comprised a complex of plain wooden buildings, connected by

THE TRANSIENCE OF PLEASURE

In the early eleventh century, an obscure daughter of a lower branch of the Fujiwara clan, Lady Murasaki, wrote a very long narrative she called the *Tale of Genji,* eclipsing all other prose writers of the age. Her book—the world's first psychological novel—was akin to the diaries kept by other ladies and recorded in exacting detail the behavior of Kyōto court society. Lady Murasaki's opportunity to observe the court's manners, superstitions, and passions had come when a fifth cousin, the illustrious Michinaga, appointed her lady-in-waiting to his daughter, Akiko, who was the consort of Emperor Ichijō.

The tale's hero is Prince Genji, son of the emperor's favorite concubine and himself a paradigm of Kyōto values. An exquisite zither player and dancer, he grumbles when govern-ment duties take time from the complicated love affairs that so absorb him. His diplomatic successes with many, varied lovers come partly from his Buddhist belief that the joys of this world are all too fleeting. At the novel's end, after Genji's death, the son born of his wife's one extramarital affair grows up to em-body this difficult truth: Prince Kaoru cannot know happiness.

Prince Genji cradles his wife's newborn son, Kaoru, wearied by the bitter certainty that the child is not his. Red tables with dishes of food have been set out to celebrate the birth, and two ladies timidly wait. The bright colors and bird's-eye perspective of this Tale of Genji *scene typify the narrative painting of this period.*

roofed walkways, and an austere garden of raked gravel and trees planted in tubs. Unlike Chinese houses, which emphasized the sharp contrast between the interior and the garden, Kyōto houses seemed to mingle with the garden. The buildings and walkways had shutters along their sides that were rolled up in warm weather to give a view of the garden outside. Walkways arched over artificial streams fed by the rivers outside the city. At parties the host floated bowls of wine down these streams. Guests who were reclining on the banks would take up the bowls, sip from them, and then return them to the stream for guests farther down. The wine put the guests into a poetic mood, and they composed verses in an atmosphere of romantic melancholy, heightened by the moonlight glimmering in the garden. In some gardens stones were set out in a line to catch the moonlight and evoke the soothing image of pale ships anchored in the black waters of a harbor.

Evening parties were the occasion for trysts, and after a party a man might come tapping at the shutter of his lover's house. "A lover's visit is the most delightful thing in the world," Sei Shōnagon wrote. "But when a man is a mere acquaintance...what a nuisance it can be!" The rooms of Japanese houses were formed by flimsy paper partitions that afforded scant privacy and provided the perfect setting for eavesdropping and romantic plots and counterplots. To guard against listeners some houses had "singing floorboards" that squeaked under the slightest footstep, betraying the presence of an eavesdropper on the other side of a partition.

The rooms in the house of a rich family were furnished sparely, but with elegance. The partitions might be of decorated paper—an art form at which the Japanese excelled, to the envy of Chinese visitors. When a lady entertained a male visitor, she spoke to him through a movable screen that completely concealed her from view. The screens were fashioned of silk and decorated with painted landscapes, with the bottom portion left loose so that the lady and her suitor might pass poems back and forth as they conversed and catch a fleeting glance of a brocade robe.

The wealthy of Kyōto amused themselves with a variety of games.

A Kyōto gentlewoman, in folded robes, has retreated from city life to read Buddhist scriptures at a mountain monastery. To her left, a tonsured monk busies himself with a tray; another, beneath a tree, meditates in a small, mist-wreathed shelter.

They staged contests for writing love letters and riddles in verse. There were incense-judging parties, at which someone mixed different scents together and his friends had to guess the ingredients. At different times of the year socialites journeyed outside the city to view cherry blossoms or hear the insects chirping. In winter they covered trees with artificial flowers to remind themselves of summer. They ordered snow piled up in shady glens, where it would last into the summer—and so remind themselves of winter.

The court calendar was crowded with religious holidays. A visit to a Buddhist temple was as much an artistic event as a religious one. Kyōto's sculptors fashioned superb wooden statues of the Buddhas and coated them with gold foil set off with white paint. The statues were housed in gilded wooden canopies with perforated designs depicting flames, flowers, clouds, and Buddhist saints. Sacred paintings showed paradise to be a wonderful place that was not unlike the court. In these paintings of heaven there was music and dancing, and all the saints wore jewels.

The most magnificent temple of Kyōto was the Hōjō-ji, commissioned by Michinaga to ensure the repose of his soul. Its dedication, in 1022, was a lavish event, restrained only a little by Michinaga's decree that court ladies could wear only six silk skirts each. The guests at the dedication passed by a mirrorlike pond in which lotus blossoms floated serenely, each blossom supporting a small statue of the Buddha. The pond reflected nets of jewels strung from shrubs along the shore and echoed the cries of peacocks parading on an island in the center. The temple itself had foundations of rock crystal, a roof beam of silver and gold, and a dazzling interior of gold, silver, and jewels.

"The world, I think is indeed my world," wrote Michinaga in a poem, "like the full moon am I, uncovered by any cloud." The private world of Michinaga, who died in 1028, was indeed unclouded. But others in Kyōto, perhaps casting a fearful eye on Michinaga's "nails and teeth," wondered what would become of their beautiful but frail world. They felt a sentiment expressed by the words *mono no aware*—a sadness at the transience of things.

TREASURES OF PAPER AND INK

A well-born Buddhist bares a lotus and the symbol A on his chest, from a scroll telling how to meditate on this first letter of the classical language of the faith, Sanskrit.

For the intensely literate aristocrats of tenth- and eleventh-century Japan, calligraphy was the highest art. Quality of line, tones of ink, and arrangement of text made an index of the calligrapher's spirituality. A perfect paper, perhaps dyed, printed with glittering mica paste, or sprinkled with gold and silver flake, was the first requirement of each calligraphic composition, for the whole beauty of an inscribed object could reveal the Buddhist vision of creation, as well as the writer's virtue. Various forms of manuscript served magical purposes—in religion, in literature, or in love. The lady or gentleman who copied or commissioned copies of Buddhist scriptures inched closer to enlightenment. And the calligraphic quality of a poem or love letter, beyond the meaning of the words, cast its spell.

Among the several syllabaries writers might choose from and the many styles of brush and ink inscription, each had its particular use. To write with Chinese characters and to study Chinese literature were the privileges of men. Women wrote on Japanese courtly subjects and in the phonetic, native syllabary, kana. Freed from the format of the Chinese, kana figures developed into a flowing script that was capable of subtle nuance.

A good hand was so identified with the cult of beauty and with religiosity that the true gentleman carried in his bosom a sheaf of papers for practicing, and the lady who abused writing brushes was beneath contempt.

In the eleventh century Kintō, a Fujiwara scholar, selected the Japanese verses he most esteemed, as Emperor Ichijō had asked. His Anthology of Poems by the Thirty-Six Immortal Poets included the page of languorous kana script (opposite) that lies on a painted collage of forested mountains with ducks flying past. The versified repartee is between the poet Ise Osuke and a former suitor who has tried to reawaken her interest after years of indifference and has sent her letters that she does not answer. He finally writes:

Were they to come back
And not wander away again,
Those tiny birds on the shore,
I am sure you would admit to having seen
The tracks they made.

And she replies:

They give no thought
To the years that have passed,
Those tiny birds on the shore,
Even were they to stay
How could they be worth seeing?

Translated by Andrew Pekarik

45

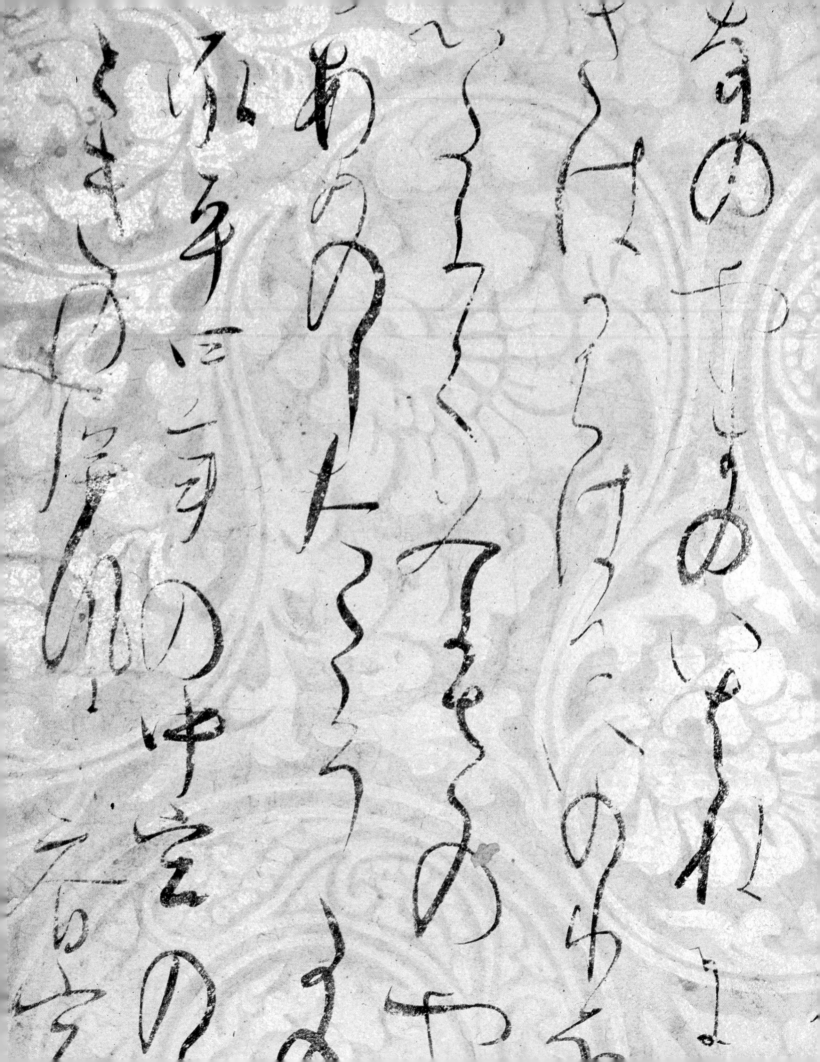

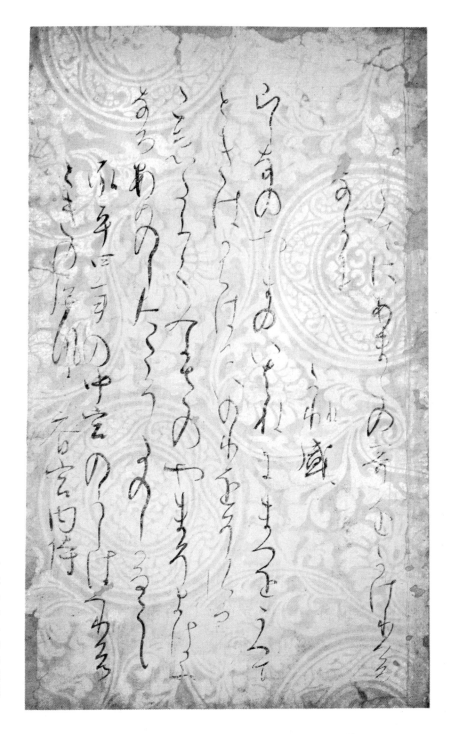

The Heian emperors had a particular enthusiasm for arranging poetry in anthologies. The page at right and in detail opposite is from a book called A Collection of Gleanings, which contains 1,300 poems. White paper, wood-block printed with arabesques of mica, provides a luminous ground for the elongated kana calligraphy attributed to Minamoto Toshiyori, a nobleman and poet. First mostly used by women, kana in time was adopted and mastered by sophisticates of the opposite sex.

The fan paper at right bears a printed, hand-colored tableau of courtly life, written over with passages from one of the earliest and most influential Buddhist scriptures, or sutras, brought from China, the *Lotus Sutra*. A couple sits at a table spread with writing and plant materials—for poets attached to each poem the leaf, flower, or twig that echoed its sentiments. The easy mingling of secular and religious themes here characterized Heian art and life.

48

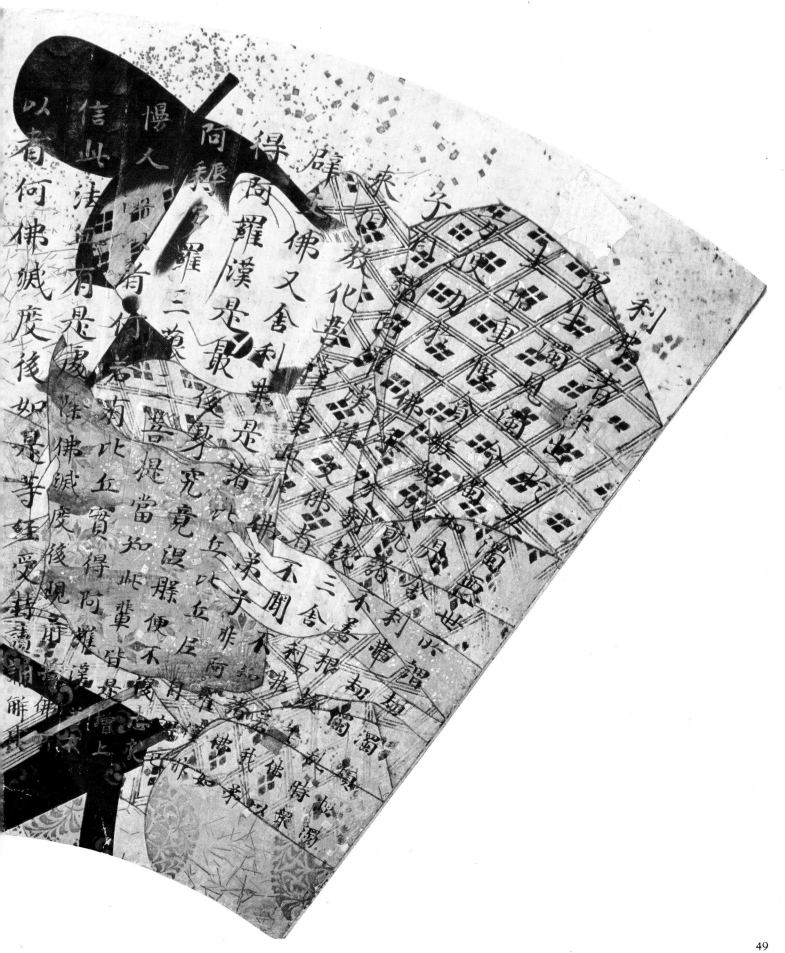

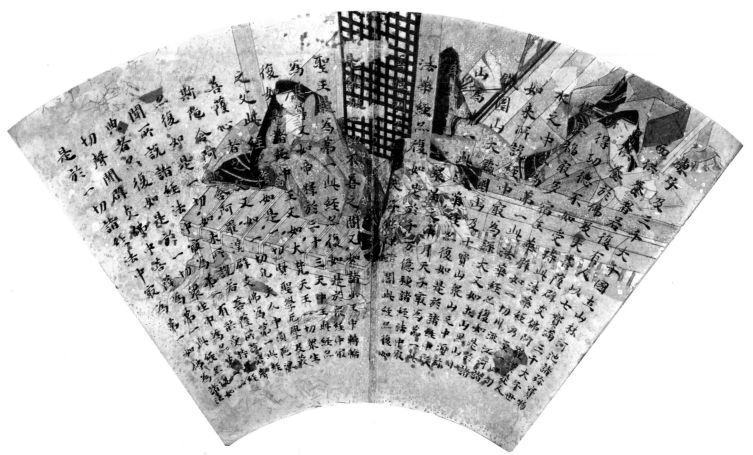

Three ladies in glowing robes and a barefoot child relax at a Heian-style dwelling with its wooden gallery and latticed shutters thrown open to nature. The fan above and in detail opposite, like those on pages 48–49 and 52–53 is covered with a Lotus Sutra text in Chinese characters, which get smaller as they descend to the fan's base. Japanese fans were coveted for their elegance. These sutra fans may have been made for a local temple ceremony that called also for offerings of incense, flowers, and jewels. Folded in half and bound into books, the inscribed fan papers counted as temple treasures.

法藥經亦復如是，於諸經中

最為其上。又如眾
星之中，月天子寂為
第一，此法華經亦復
如是，於千萬億種諸
經法中，最為照明。此
經亦復如是，能除
諸闇。

後如是於諸經
中

聖王最為
是。為弟一，此
如帝釋於
王天又如大梵天
王，一切眾
生之父，此
經亦復如
是，一切賢
聖、學、無學
及發菩薩
心者

又如一切凡
夫人中，須陀
洹、斯陀含、
阿那含、阿
羅漢、辟支佛
為第一，此
經亦復如
是，一切如來
所說，若菩薩、
若佛所說
諸經法中，
最為第一。
有能受持
是經典者，亦
復如是，於
一切眾生
中亦為第一

又如諸小
王中，轉輪
聖王最為
第一，此經亦
復如是，於
眾經中最
為其尊。又如
帝釋於三
十三天中
王，此經亦復
如是，諸經
中王

見聞讀誦
如說修行

之父此經
復如是
者
菩薩心

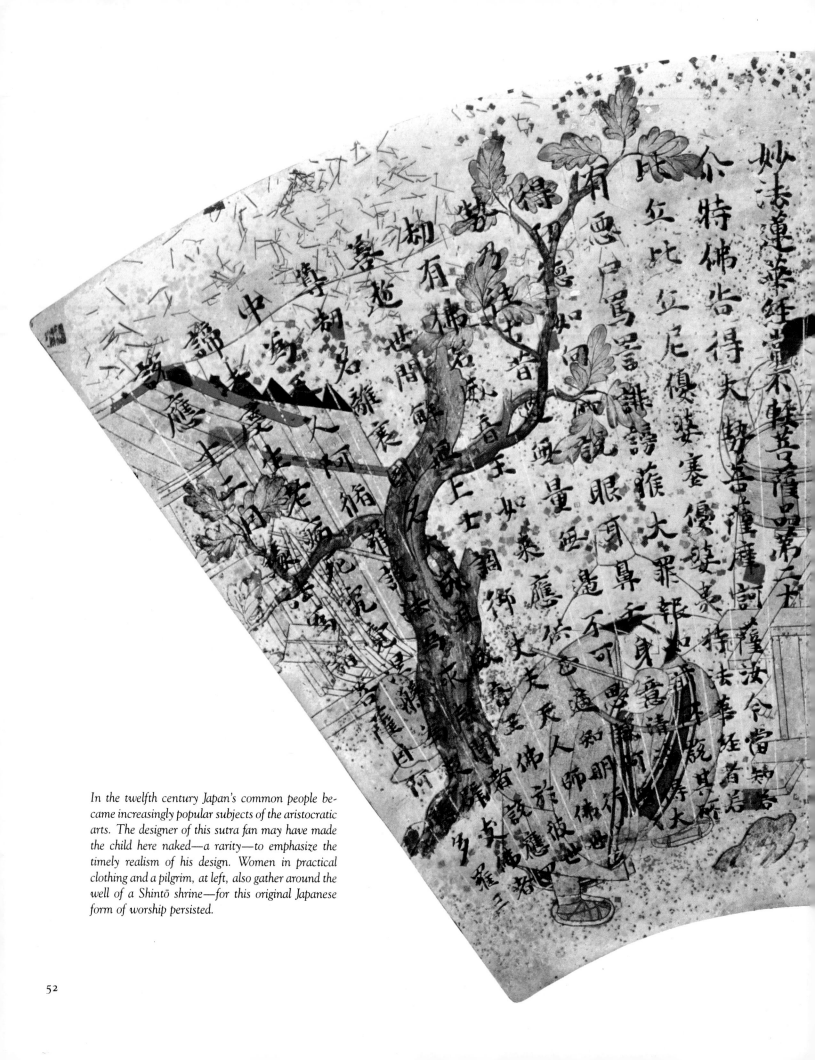

In the twelfth century Japan's common people became increasingly popular subjects of the aristocratic arts. The designer of this sutra fan may have made the child here naked—a rarity—to emphasize the timely realism of his design. Women in practical clothing and a pilgrim, at left, also gather around the well of a Shintō shrine—for this original Japanese form of worship persisted.

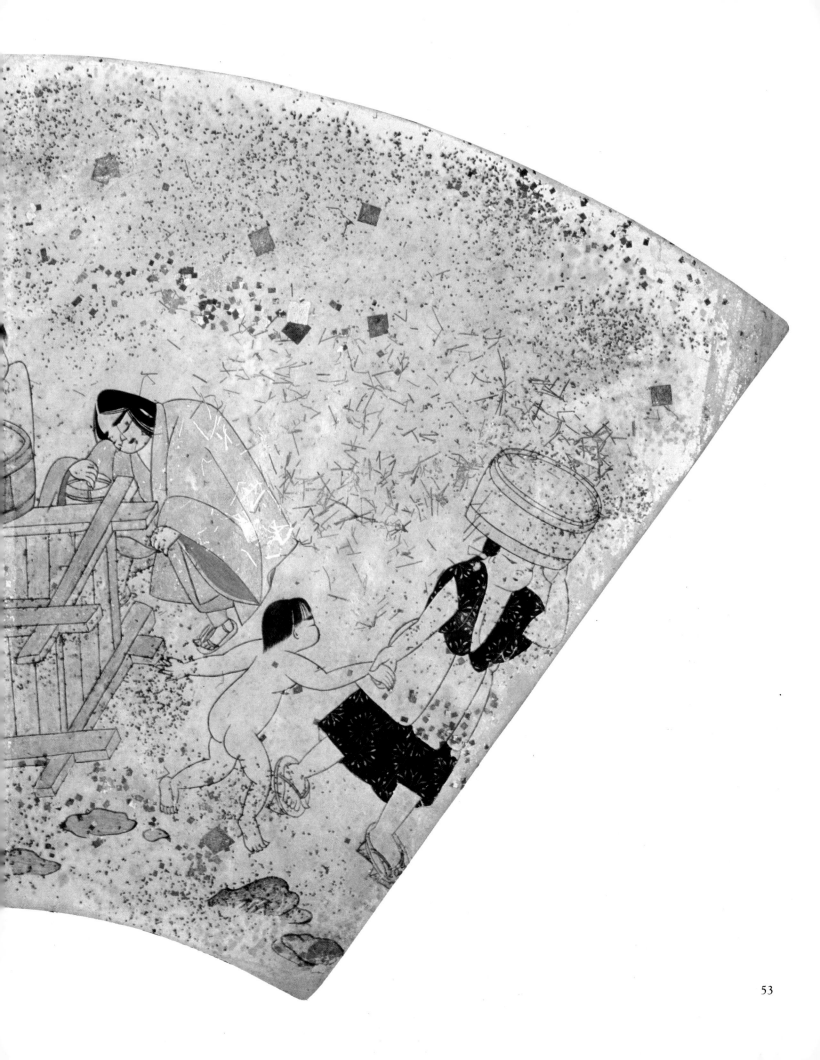

大方廣佛華嚴經後慈分一卷

三藏法師提雲般若奉　制譯

如是我聞一時佛在王舍城鷲峯山中與

无量大菩薩衆俱旀勒菩薩摩訶薩而爲

上首尒時東方有十億梵天皆徍慈心來詣

佛所頂礼佛足以衆妙供養旀佛供養畢已

大般若經卷第七十八

神護寺

大方廣佛華嚴經修慈分

Indigo-blue paper and gold and silver inks were the stuff of many of the twelfth-century sutra scrolls produced by professional sutra artists at the command of an emperor or noble. The scrolls here are copies of two different sutras. The rolled scroll opposite contains the Greater Sutra of the Perfection of Wisdom, which monks read aloud to drive evil forces from Japan. The open scroll at left recounts a famous colloquy between the Buddha and his followers at Vulture Peak, a mountain in India. In the frontispiece the Buddha sits on a lotus throne and the vulture-shaped mountain behind him is crested with trees. The Chinese text is written in tidy, traditional characters, as is the red seal of the Kyōto temple that received the scroll from a generous emperor.

III

YORITOMO THE FIRST SHOGUN

THE AGE OF STEEL

The twelfth century was the age of the sword. By mid-century, the elegant courtiers of imperial Kyōto no longer held sway over the land. The mighty of Japan were the samurai—warriors who were deadly masters of the sword. The samurai disdained luxuries, but they did possess, and cherish, beautiful treasures—their armor and their swords. The suits of armor tightly laced of iron, silk, and leather were masterpieces intended to fill the beholder with terror. The scabbards of some swords gleamed with gold. A carefully wrought scene from the life of a mythical hero often adorned the hilt. But the real beauty, and the mystique, of a samurai's sword lay in its blade. A graceful arc of steel, pure and strong, the blade was the slender, flashing line between life and death.

Two samurai clans, the Taira and the Minamoto, dominated the age. Each produced an important leader: Taira Kiyomori, who lived from 1118 to 1181, and Minamoto Yoritomo, from 1147 to 1199. Kiyomori was audacious enough to ally himself with an emperor, fight the sovereign's battles, and then use his high position at court to

Yoritomo, head of the Minamoto clan and Japan's first shogun, replacing the emperor as chief of state, rose to power about 1185. Here he wears formal court robes.

usurp the emperor's power. But Yoritomo, by far, was the towering figure of the century. A statesman of genius, Yoritomo sought to shatter the age-old pretense that court alliances and intrigues could govern the land. Yoritomo intended to rule purely by the sword, as the shogun, or "generalissimo." He loathed the very trappings of the court. Though Kiyomori and Yoritomo were a generation apart, their lives intersected fatefully. The Taira and the Minamoto eventually fought each other in a series of epic battles, collectively known as the Gempei War, that lasted from 1180 to 1185. Their feuds were personal, but vengeance was not the only motive; indeed, the mastery of Japan was the prize.

The rise to power of the samurai clans was sharply ironic. The Taira and Minamoto clans, whose might overshadowed the emperor's in the second half of the twelfth century, had been founded by imperial castoffs. In the ninth century a number of princes were forced out of the imperial family and stripped of their birthrights simply because the emperors could not afford to support all their descendants in princely splendor. The princes gravitated to Japan's northern and eastern frontiers, where they and their descendants made a new life for themselves in the wilderness and became hardy fighting men from centuries of battling the indigenous peoples. These frontiersmen formed the Taira and Minamoto clans—families of warriors who called themselves samurai.

The word "samurai" meant "one who serves," signifying the loyalty of the warrior to his emperor, his chief, and his clan. In the twelfth century, after Yoritomo decreed that only sons of samurai could join the brotherhood, the samurai became an elite class. A boy destined to become a samurai learned to handle a wooden sword as soon as he was old enough to grasp a hilt. When he was five the boy's elders dressed him in armor and thrust a steel sword into his belt. Young warriors practiced fencing, archery, horsemanship, and ju-jitsu—the art of fighting without weapons. Their teachers did more than simply drill the fledgling warriors in military skills; they imparted the virtues of a samurai. For example, when a boy was cooking or sleeping, his master would come up behind him and

Armed with bows and swords, samurai—the mighty warriors of feudal Japan—swarm on both sides of a stone wall built between 1274 and 1281 to ward off attacks from mainland Mongols. This scene and the one on pages 60–61 are from a thirteenth-century painted narrative scroll.

strike him with a wooden sword in order to teach constant vigilance. From long fasts and barefoot marches through the snow, the boy learned endurance and a cardinal samurai virtue, *fudōshin*, the "immobility of the heart," an inner calm that endured even in the most desperate battle.

Samurai had to take a vow to ignore the Buddhist law against the taking of life; and though their business was to break this law, victorious warriors often felt a keen guilt at the death they inflicted. According to one well-known story, a samurai captured an enemy in battle and pulled off his helmet to behead him. He saw that his enemy was just a boy, so he held back. Realizing that the boy would eventually die at the executioner's hands—the fate of the captured—the samurai lopped off the boy's head with a single stroke to give him an honorable death on the field of battle. But then the samurai threw away his sword and spent the rest of his life as a monk to atone for the killing.

Nor did a samurai have any hesitation about taking his own life to preserve his honor. To a samurai trained in immobility of the heart, death was "lighter than a feather." The prescribed ritual of suicide, called seppuku, was the ultimate test of a warrior's character. The word "seppuku" means "to cut the bowels." In this ritual the samurai knelt on a mat and laid a short sword in front of him. He placed his sleeves under his knees so that his corpse would fall forward instead of backward, which was dishonorable. He took up the sword, plunged it into the left side of his abdomen, drew it slowly to the right and then up. At this point a companion standing by with a sword leaped forward and beheaded the samurai to end his agony. Only a samurai had the privilege of committing suicide in this way.

On the frontier, where the Taira and Minamoto samurai were bred, loyalties were clear. A warrior knew his chief. And the warrior's duty to protect the chief's clan and lands was plain. The Taira and Minamoto samurai who served as peacekeepers in Kyōto breathed in a different atmosphere. In that city of schemers, of palace plots and counterplots, loyalty was a wisp. The samurai's first loyalty was ostensibly to the emperor, but the obsessive scheming of the Fujiwara courtiers made it unclear who the emperor actually was. The Fujiwara had instituted the custom of easing an adult emperor into retirement to make way for a boy-sovereign who could be manipulated by the regent. In the twelfth century the supposedly retired emperors—sometimes several of them at once—maintained their own courts and governments that existed side by side with the bureaucracy of the reigning emperor. The Taira and Minamoto chiefs looked on this tangle of court and shadow court with mounting cynicism. So when Emperor Go-Shirakawa called upon the Taira chief Kiyomori to support him in court disputes, Kiyomori used the invitation to his own ends.

Kiyomori defeated Go-Shirakawa's rivals in two celebrated battles in and around Kyōto, in 1156 and 1160. The second battle clearly pitted the Taira clan against the Minamoto for the first time. The leader of the Minamoto at that time was Yoshitomo, the father of Yoritomo, (then fourteen years old), and of other sons. The Minamoto samurai chose a moment when Kiyomori was on a pilgrimage far away from Kyōto and launched a ferocious attack on the Imperial Palace, which they burned to the ground. But Kiyomori came back; his sons led a thousand Taira samurai against Yoshitomo and his men and completely routed them. Yoshitomo, with three of his sons, fled into the mountains.

Yoshitomo's flight did not save him. One of his trusted friends turned traitor and stabbed him while he was in his bath. Now, just when Kiyomori could have crushed the leading family of the Minamoto completely, he succumbed both to kindheartedness and to lust. He banished Yoshitomo's eldest son, Yoritomo, rather than kill him, and he spared Yoshitomo's infant son, Yoshitsune, because the boy's mother was beautiful. She agreed to become Kiyomori's mistress on the condition that Yoshitsune as well as her two other sons be sent to a monastery. The children spared by Kiyomori would grow up to topple the house of Taira.

"Not to be a Taira is not to be a man!" was the triumphant cry of Kiyomori's clan after their victory. With no one to oppose him in the field, he forced the emperor Go-Shirakawa to appoint him chancel-

A violent storm drove back the first Mongol invasion in 1274, but seven years later the Mongols again set sail for Japan. This time the samurai attacked the enemy fleet before it even reached shore. Here, Japanese warriors attack the Mongol leaders' boat.

lor of the realm. He handed out Minamoto lands to his samurai, who rapidly acquired upper-class tastes. At a site overlooking the Inland Sea at Itsukushima, Kiyomori rebuilt a grandiose Shintō shrine, open at the sides and with long corridors stretching over the waters of the sea. The Japanese had by now reconciled Shintō beliefs with Buddhism, and Kiyomori donated an exquisite set of Buddhist scrolls to the shrine—perhaps the finest ever seen in Japan—and the cases that held the scrolls were treasures in themselves: darkened bronze boxes decorated with dragons and clouds of silver and gold. Along with their rich religious gifts, Kiyomori and his samurai deposited their armor at the shrine as offerings of thanks for their victory over the Minamoto.

But the years passed, and the sons of Yoshitomo grew to manhood with a bitter hatred of the Taira. Yoshitsune, virtually a prisoner in the monastery where Kiyomori had sent him as an infant, escaped at the age of fifteen and fled to the far north of Japan, where he spent his youth training himself to become the greatest swordsman in northern Japan. Then he went in search of his brother.

Yoritomo, banished to the eastern province of Izu, had not forgotten that his father had been the chief of a mighty clan and resolved that one day he would wield even greater power. Through a high-placed friend in Kyōto, Yoritomo kept up with the intrigues of the Taira court. He slowly gathered allies from among the scattered remnants of the Minamoto clan and from among Taira landowners, some of whom hated their powerful relatives.

In 1180, twenty years after his father's death, Yoritomo raised the white battle standard of the Minamoto clan and took to the field— the Gempei War had begun. In an early skirmish the Taira defeated Yoritomo's small force, but they could not put a stop to the burgeoning revolt. Yoshitsune was among the Minamoto samurai who flocked to Yoritomo's standard. In Kyōto Kiyomori was enraged at the sudden uprising, but was fatally ill. On his deathbed, in 1181, Kiyomori made his samurai vow to kill Yoritomo.

Yoritomo began to set up a government, called the *Bakufu*, or "tent government," reflecting the stern military discipline Yoritomo believed in. For his capital he chose a place called Kamakura, on the edge of Sagami Bay, about forty miles east of Mount Fuji. In setting up his government before the Minamoto army had won a single major battle, Yoritomo demonstrated the boundless self-confidence and determination of a visionary. But he had none of the visionary's delusions. He was ruthless, cold, and suspicious, even of his closest comrades. When one of his cousins, a successful general, appeared to waver in his loyalty, Yoritomo had him hunted down and killed.

In just three years Minamoto armies swept the Taira armies from eastern Japan and took Kyōto. The Taira fled the capital, taking with them the five-year-old reigning emperor, Antoku, and the sacred imperial regalia—the sword, the gem, and the mirror, handed down from Japan's first emperor. Far from defeated, the Taira took refuge on the islands of Shikoku and Kyūshū , and in the western provinces of Honshū. The Taira also controlled the routes across the Inland Sea, whose waters Taira ships had plied for a century. Early in 1184 some five thousand Taira troops were in a formidable position on the northern shore of the Inland Sea in Settsu province. Mountains protected them on the north, fortifications on the west, and a forest on the east. A Minamoto army under Yoshitsune attacked the Taira stronghold from two directions. The main thrust was aimed at the forest. But Yoshitsune, with seventy-five chosen men, planned to surprise the Taira by pushing through the supposedly impenetrable mountains on the north. And his plan worked. While the Taira were occupied with the main attack, the irrepressible Yoshitsune led a gallop down a steep hillside into the Taira camp and torched it. About a thousand Taira were killed or captured, though three thousand escaped by ship. A Taira commander, Tadanori, was killed, but won immortality by composing a poem, which he hid in his helmet, in premonition of his defeat and death:

> Twilight upon my path,
> And for my inn tonight
> The shadow of a tree,
> And for my host, a flower.

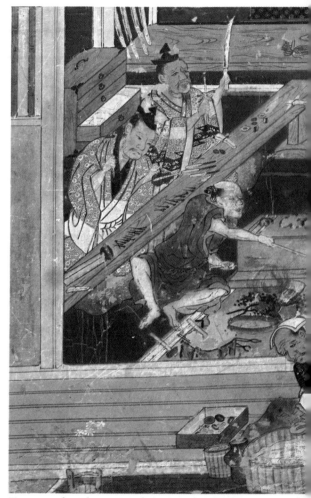

Two swordsmiths, upper left, put the finishing touches on hilts as others heat a blade and finish sword guards; a woman brews tea. The forging of a samurai sword was a sacred activity, and a workshop such as this a veritable shrine.

This victory cleared the Taira from much of Honshū, but left intact their strongholds on Kyūshū and Shikoku, where the Taira were holding the boy-emperor Antoku at a seaside fortress. Ignorant of naval matters, Yoshitsune commandeered a small fleet on the Inland Sea. In April 1185 he led the Minamoto navy in the decisive battle of the war, which was fought in a strait between Kyūshū and Honshū, near a village named Danno-ura. The entire Taira navy gathered in the hope of crushing the fleet of the Minamoto, which had been hastily assembled. This battle, like all others fought in Japan before the advent of artillery, was mainly a battle of archers followed by hand-to-hand combat, with the ships serving as floating platforms. The two fleets pulled up alongside each other, with the Taira ships between the shore and the Minamoto. The Taira commanders counted on a brief battle, planning to rout the Minamoto before high tide. But Yoshitsune made up for his naval inexperience with an inspired tactical move: he ordered his archers to shoot only at the Taira helmsmen. Soon many of the Taira ships were weaving out of control, their helmsmen shot dead. Then the tide literally and figuratively turned. One Taira squadron joined the Minamoto, and then, as the tide in the strait ebbed and the rushing current drove the Taira fleet close to shore, the Minamoto broke up the Taira formations. In the ensuing panic, the boy-emperor drowned, and the imperial regalia was lost. Yoshitsune's divers later recovered the mirror and the gem, but not the sword.

The victory at Danno-ura made Yoritomo the overlord of Japan; but the man who made that victory possible received a bitter reward. Yoshitsune had become a favorite of the courtiers at Kyōto. He told war stories at parties and was lionized as the hero who had single-handedly defeated the Taira. Yoritomo viewed his brother's popularity with alarm and refused to see him. From outside Kamakura, Yoshitsune wrote a piteous letter to his brother, begging for a reconciliation. "Here I am, weeping crimson tears in vain at your displeasure.... The bond of our blood-brotherhood is sundered." Yoritomo responded by sending men to kill him. At length, hounded by his brother and hemmed in by troops, the hero of the

TEXT CONTINUED ON PAGE 70

THE SOUL
OF A SWORD

Slung from the belts of armored warriors, samurai swords defined the essence of the men who so proudly wore them. In single shafts of steel the *kaji,* master swordsmiths of ancient Japan, created superb weapons that were also emblems of valor, authority, and strength. Whether a long, curved katana (above), a *tachi* blade (pages 66–67), or a short *tantō* dagger (pages 68–69), these Japanese swords became in legend "the living soul of the samuari."

Beginning in the twelfth century when the samurai were in the service of clan lords, no greater treasures than finely forged swords existed in Japan. No stash of silver or gold, nor any parcel of land could compare in value with these blades. The swords on these pages, by such masters as Gō-Yoshihiro, Masamune, and Yoshimitsu, are among the finest ever made.

In forges located in central Japan—a region rich in iron sand—swordsmiths refined the craft that the twelfth-century emperor Go-Toba had decreed worthy of princes. The kaji and his assistants began their work with a ritual cleansing of body and mind. They dressed in white, adhered to strict diets, and forsook worldly pleasures that might distract them from their lethal masterpieces. After hanging strips of rice paper throughout the forge to ward off evil spirits, the

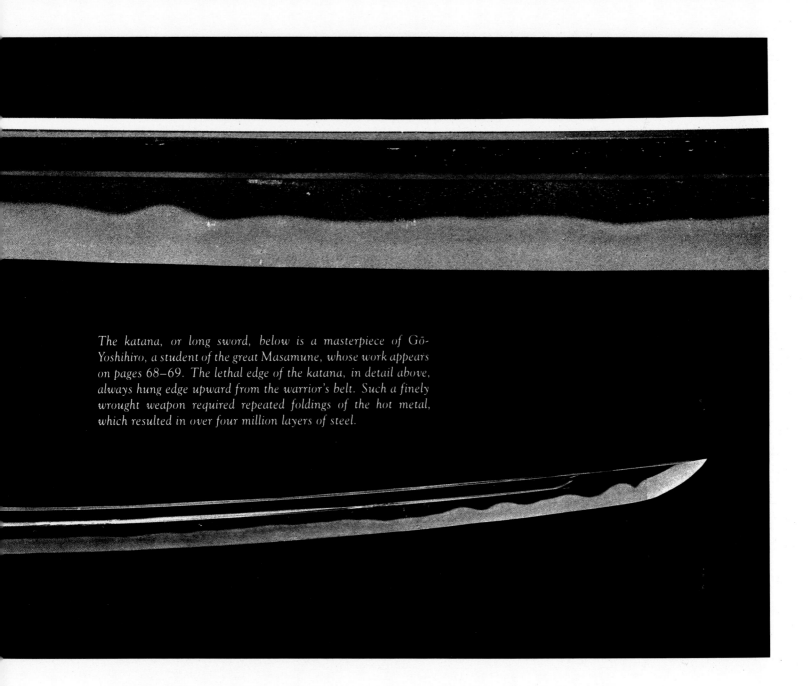

The katana, or long sword, below is a masterpiece of Gō-Yoshihiro, a student of the great Masamune, whose work appears on pages 68–69. The lethal edge of the katana, in detail above, always hung edge upward from the warrior's belt. Such a finely wrought weapon required repeated foldings of the hot metal, which resulted in over four million layers of steel.

sword makers began what could be two years of exacting labor on one sword.

Placing bars of crude metal in a charcoal furnace—one craftsman advised heating the iron until it turns "the color of the moon about to set out on its journey on a June or July evening"—the smith then hammered out impurities from the iron. Then he pounded the bar flat and folded it and hammered it again and again, plunging the glowing billets into water between the fiery beatings. Starting with twenty-two pounds of metal, a swordsmith would produce a blade of only three or four pounds, rendering from the iron several million fine layers of steel. The kaji paid closest attention to the sword's edge and the *hamon*, or grain—the wavy line from the tang (the hilt end) to the point. Variations in the hamon enhanced the beauty and strength of the sword. Having achieved the proper degree of hardness, flexibility, and sharpness—as well as a beautiful texture—the smith gave the blade a final bath and then often incised his signature into it.

After furnishing the polished blade with a *tsuba*, or guard, as well as a hilt, a scabbard, and other mountings, the smith presented his creation to the samurai, who might name it—as if the sword had a life of its own.

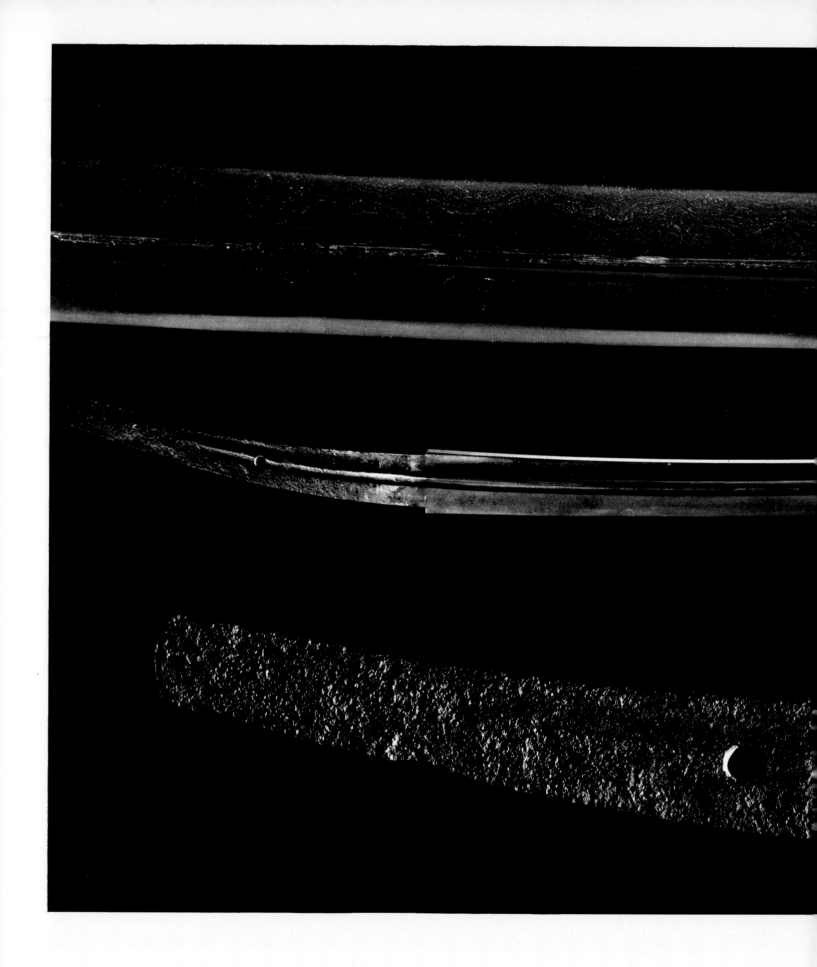

This prized ancient tachi—in three views—belonged to the Taira, the clan whose defeat by the Minamoto gave rise to the shogunate in the twelfth century. According to legend Amakuni, the eighth-century smith who made this blade, spent thirty sleepless days forging the very first sword. Both the point (top) and the tang (bottom) of the sword (center) are in detail.

The double-edged ken above, *the oldest kind of Japanese blade, is the work of Yoshimitsu, one of the premiere swordsmiths of Kyōto. Through many fiery renderings of the metal he achieved the lighter shading around the edge, the hardest part of the steel, which gives the sword its treasured grain.*

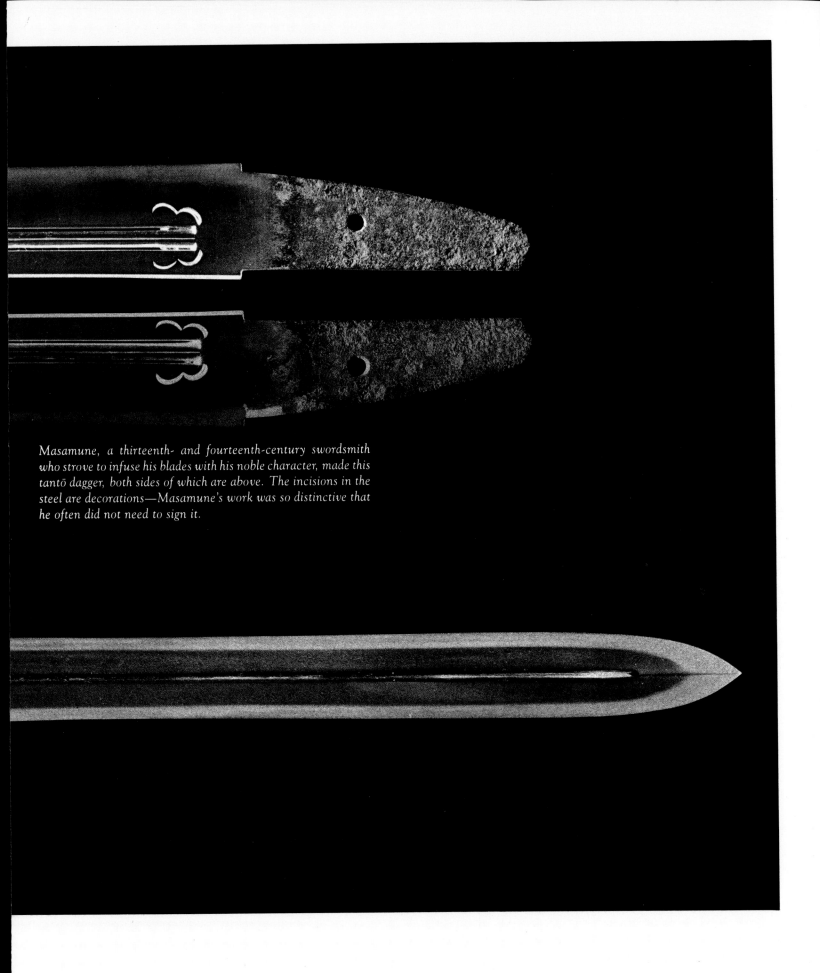

Masamune, a thirteenth- and fourteenth-century swordsmith who strove to infuse his blades with his noble character, made this tantō dagger, both sides of which are above. The incisions in the steel are decorations—Masamune's work was so distinctive that he often did not need to sign it.

TEXT CONTINUED FROM PAGE 63

Gempei War slew his family and committed suicide.

Now Yoritomo ruled alone. Though he was careful to portray himself as the loyal agent and protector of the emperor, he made it plain that the emperor had no power. Yoritomo seized the lands of the defeated Taira, parceled them out to his soldiers, and made those soldiers his vassals. He appointed these vassals to the important administrative posts throughout the country. Every estate was assigned a manager to collect Yoritomo's taxes and administer the laws. The court bureaucracy faded to insignificance, while the power base of Japan shifted to the Bakufu at Kamakura. The final act in the transfer of power came in the year 1192, when the thirteen-year-old sovereign, Go-Toba, named Yoritomo the shogun.

For all his success, Yoritomo's life ended in tragedy. In 1199, while riding in a procession at the dedication of a new bridge, he abruptly fell from his horse and died—for no apparent reason. The suddenness of his fall stirred a rumor that the ghost of Yoshitsune had appeared before Yoritomo. In terror and in guilt, people said, Yoritomo had swooned.

Nevertheless, the government Yoritomo had established at Kamakura ruled Japan honestly and well—so well that even the Bakufu's tax system earned a measure of respect from the peasants. Most important, the Bakufu was frugal. It eschewed luxurious palaces, ceremonies, and personal adornments—in short, it was the opposite of the imperial capital. Indeed the regime proved to be the bulwark that saved Japan from conquest by one of the most powerful and ruthless military machines in history—the Mongol empire. By the middle of the thirteenth century, the Mongols had conquered much of China, had absorbed Korea almost effortlessly, and were casting a greedy eye on Japan. The leader of the Mongols, Kublai Khan, sent ambassadors to Japan in 1268 demanding that Japan submit to him or face invasion. Panic-stricken, the court at Kyōto was inclined to negotiate; but the Bakufu stood firm, sent the envoys away empty-handed, and prepared for war.

In 1274 a Mongol fleet made up of some eight hundred Korean vessels, carrying thirty thousand men, set sail for Japan and landed in

DRESSED TO KILL

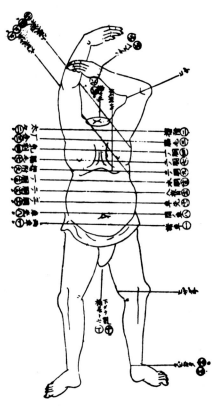

Samurai occasionally tested their new swords on unfortunate passersby or often on the corpses of criminals. This illustration from a treatise on swords and armor shows the choicest cuts of combat. Each incision had a special name: the ''pair of wheels'' was a cut across the lower abdomen and was the most difficult; ''cutting the sleeve'' was the relatively easy maneuver of slicing off a hand.

After the military government of the shogun established itself at Kamakura late in the twelfth century, the samurai, who rose to fight Japan's feudal wars, devised and adhered to the bushido, originally an unwritten code defining the honorable "way of the warrior." The bushido also linked the samurai so completely to his swords that he could scarcely exist without them.

Though the samurai were usually servants of feudal barons—the word itself is based on an ideogram for "one who serves"—they towered over other castes. Farmers, merchants, and artisans shuddered in the presence of these terrifying warriors. Their privileges even included the right to dismember any commoner who failed to show them proper respect. Most samurai were completely dependent on their masters for rations and shelter, but the frugality of their lives only intensified their concentration on fighting: dressing for battle (as the warrior does at right) and practicing deadly blows with swords (diagramed opposite) meant more to the samurai than personal well-being.

As bloody as it might be, samurai combat was governed by strict rules of etiquette requiring that warriors first address their opponents and exchange credentials before attempting to decapitate one another. A proper samurai perfumed his helmet so that his head—if taken in the fight—would not foul the victor's saddlebag.

Whether striking out at a passing peasant to test a new blade, bisecting an enemy in a single motion, or plunging a sword into his own belly to rectify cowardice or some other disgrace, the samurai lived each day by his sword, and one day might die by it.

1

The samurai in these woodcuts dresses for battle, his mood intensifying for combat as he moves from cotton undergarments to armor. First the warrior belts his kimono (1), then he ties pantaloons around his waist (2) and pulls on sleeves of mail (3). Next he secures his heavy, pleated sheath (4) and, finally, dons a scowling mask of iron (5). Each piece is shown both by itself and on the model in these illustrations from a manual on samurai armor.

4

3

5

Each samurai clan employed its own armorers, who, like those above, worked solely on casting, polishing, and decorating their warriors' gear. This screen from the seventeenth century shows armorers at work.

the bay of Hakozaki in Kyūshū. A nearby garrison spread the alarm throughout Kyūshū, bringing the samurai galloping to meet the invaders. The ensuing battle lasted just one day. A storm blew up, and the Korean sea pilots persuaded the Mongol commanders to reembark and set sail lest the fleet be thrown against the shore. When the samurai arrived at the field in the morning, they saw the final stragglers of the enemy fleet leaving the bay.

Any hope that Kublai Khan might abandon his plans for conquest was dashed by the arrival of more envoys, this time demanding that the emperor himself appear before the khan in Peking. The answer was "no" in strong terms: the ambassadors were executed. Kublai Khan established an "office for the chastisement of Japan" that stripped the hills of Korea bare in order to build another fleet. In 1281, seven years after the first attack, a massive armada of more than 3,500 vessels and 140,000 men sailed for Japan. Fortunately the Bakufu had used the seven-year breathing space between the invasions wisely; they built a stone wall along the shore at Hakozaki Bay, in addition to a fleet of small, maneuverable vessels that were manned by pirates.

The Mongols landed at Hakozaki Bay and along the nearby shores in June 1281. For seven weeks the battle raged, as Mongol and Chinese troops tried to outflank the defensive wall, with no success. The samurai fought desperately, and the small Japanese ships sowed havoc among the slow, bulky Mongol transports.

The brave resistance of the samurai held the Mongols to their beachhead until August—the hurricane season. On August 15 a typhoon suddenly roared in from the west and blew for two days. It smashed the Mongol fleet onto the shore, where the samurai made short work of the stunned survivors. Many of the ships that managed to escape foundered on the mountainous seas. The Japanese believed that the gods had sent the typhoon, and so they called it kamikaze, "the divine wind." The elements had struck the decisive blow, but what saved Japan was the indomitable courage of the men of the sword, clad in their demonic, brilliantly colored armor and their helmets with gilded horns. It was the samurai's finest hour.

SILK AND IRON

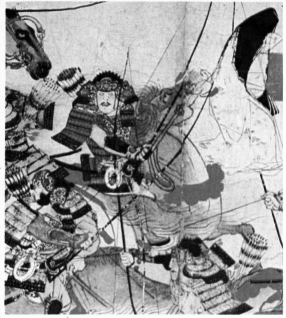

Armored warriors of the Minamoto clan raise swords and bows in the midst of a battle in Kyōto. This scene is from a mid-thirteenth-century scroll.

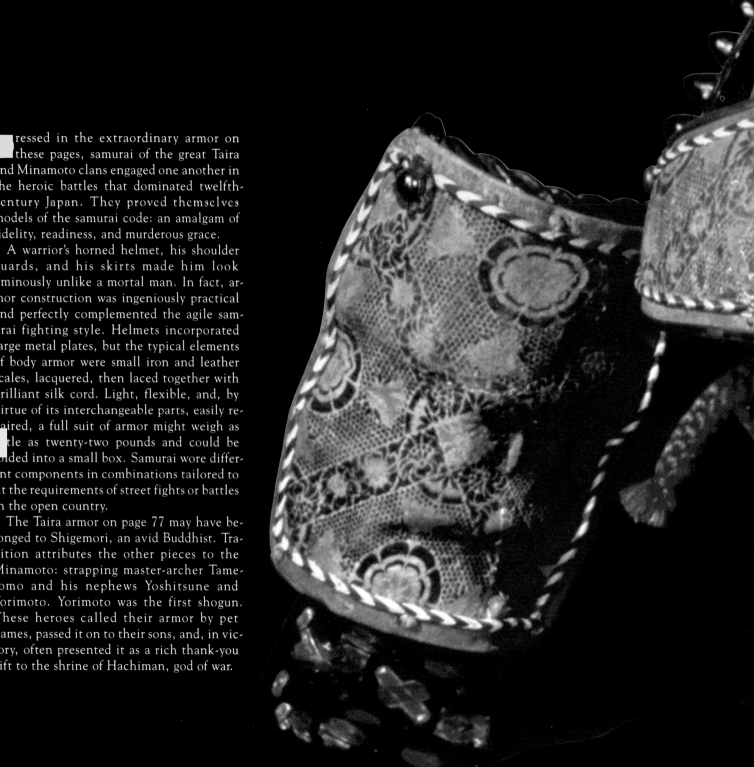

ressed in the extraordinary armor on these pages, samurai of the great Taira and Minamoto clans engaged one another in the heroic battles that dominated twelfth-century Japan. They proved themselves models of the samurai code: an amalgam of fidelity, readiness, and murderous grace.

A warrior's horned helmet, his shoulder guards, and his skirts made him look ominously unlike a mortal man. In fact, armor construction was ingeniously practical and perfectly complemented the agile samurai fighting style. Helmets incorporated large metal plates, but the typical elements of body armor were small iron and leather scales, lacquered, then laced together with brilliant silk cord. Light, flexible, and, by virtue of its interchangeable parts, easily repaired, a full suit of armor might weigh as little as twenty-two pounds and could be folded into a small box. Samurai wore different components in combinations tailored to fit the requirements of street fights or battles in the open country.

The Taira armor on page 77 may have belonged to Shigemori, an avid Buddhist. Tradition attributes the other pieces to the Minamoto: strapping master-archer Tametomo and his nephews Yoshitsune and Yorimoto. Yorimoto was the first shogun. These heroes called their armor by pet names, passed it on to their sons, and, in victory, often presented it as a rich thank-you gift to the shrine of Hachiman, god of war.

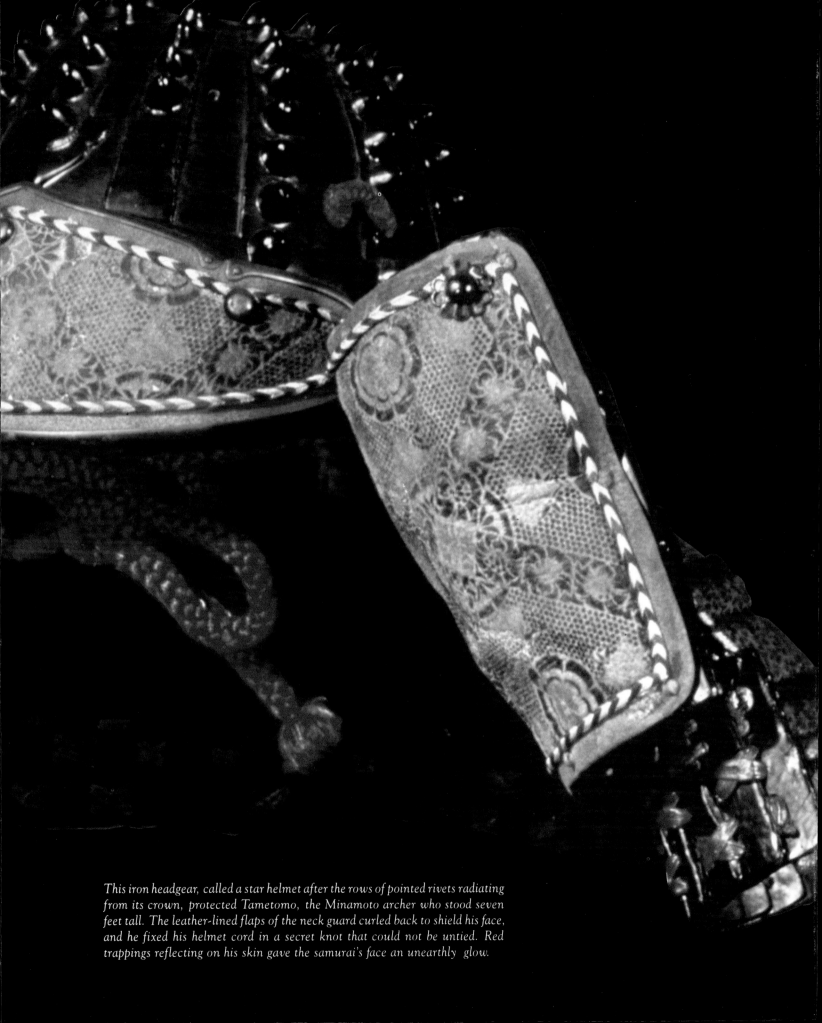

This iron headgear, called a star helmet after the rows of pointed rivets radiating from its crown, protected Tametomo, the Minamoto archer who stood seven feet tall. The leather-lined flaps of the neck guard curled back to shield his face, and he fixed his helmet cord in a secret knot that could not be untied. Red trappings reflecting on his skin gave the samurai's face an unearthly glow.

After establishing his sovereignty at Kamakura, Yoritomo dedicated the classic horseman's armor above, with its four-part skirt, to his clan shrine. The great corselet, decorated with lions frolicking on a flowery field, covered the stomach, which the Japanese thought was the source of all emotion.

The armor opposite belonged to the Taira warrior Shigemori, who, like other samurai in Kyōto, apparently had a taste for rich trimmings. The two appendages on the breast prevented vital armor cords—and armpits as well—from being slashed. The left-hand one is a solid plate, for as an archer took aim he particularly exposed his left, or bow-shooting, side.

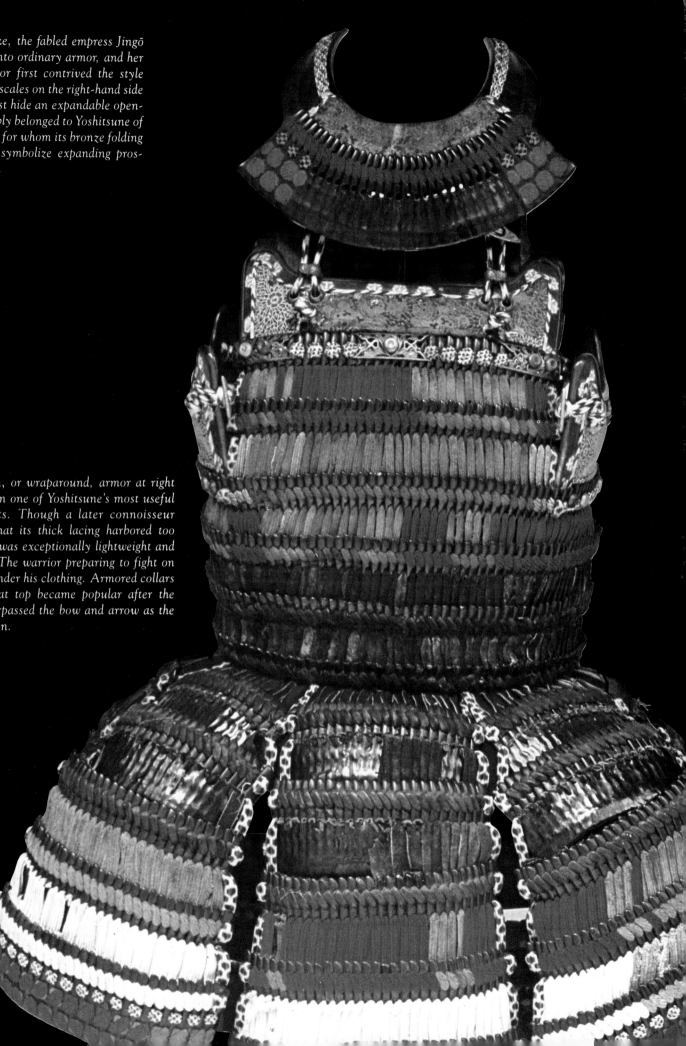

Pregnant but warlike, the fabled empress Jingō could not squeeze into ordinary armor, and her resourceful counselor first contrived the style opposite. The laced scales on the right-hand side of the corselet's waist hide an expandable opening. This one probably belonged to Yoshitsune of the Minamoto clan, for whom its bronze folding fan insignia would symbolize expanding prospects and good luck.

The haramaki, or wraparound, armor at right may have been one of Yoshitsune's most useful accoutrements. Though a later connoisseur complained that its thick lacing harbored too many lice, it was exceptionally lightweight and close-fitting. The warrior preparing to fight on foot wore it under his clothing. Armored collars like the one at top became popular after the sword had surpassed the bow and arrow as the noblest weapon.

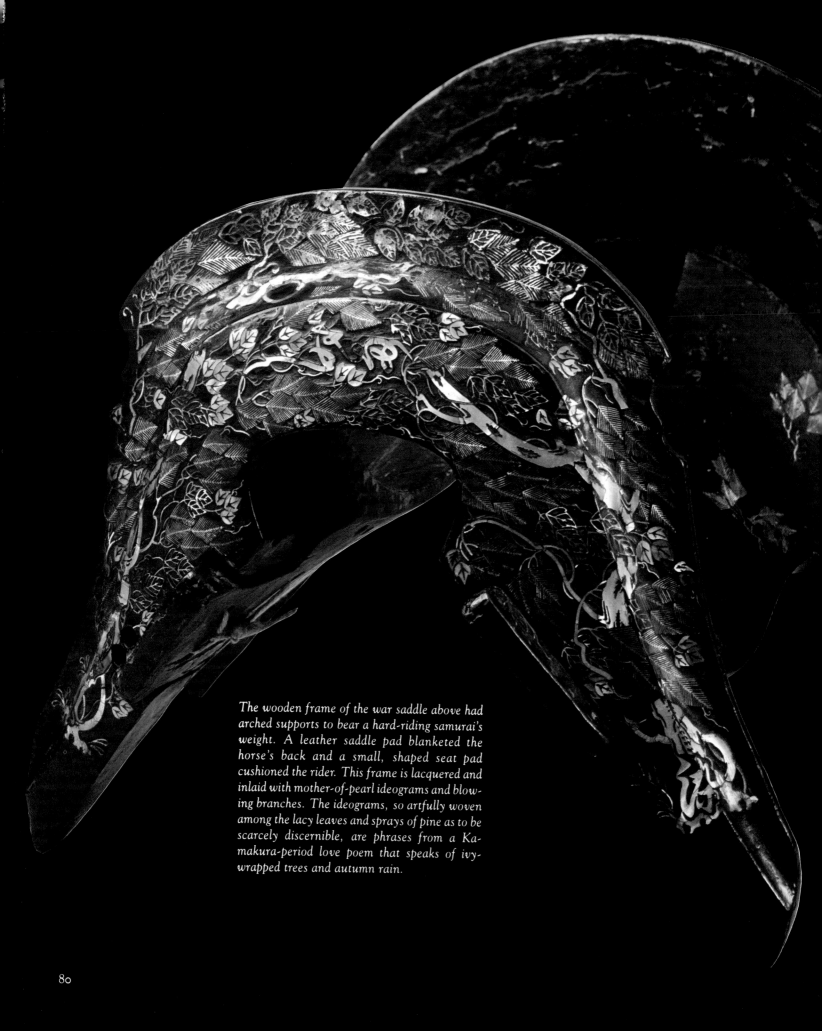

The wooden frame of the war saddle above had arched supports to bear a hard-riding samurai's weight. A leather saddle pad blanketed the horse's back and a small, shaped seat pad cushioned the rider. This frame is lacquered and inlaid with mother-of-pearl ideograms and blowing branches. The ideograms, so artfully woven among the lacy leaves and sprays of pine as to be scarcely discernible, are phrases from a Kamakura-period love poem that speaks of ivy-wrapped trees and autumn rain.

Banks of gilt flowers cover the hand guards (bottom) and round elbow shields of these chain mail sleeves, perhaps worn by Yoshitsune in his last years. A spotted butterfly, harbinger of gentleness and elegance, floats on each hand guard.

In the mid-fourteenth century, toward the end of the first epoch of samurai rule, an armorer made the ceremonial suit opposite and in detail at left. The chrysanthemum, which the Japanese loved for its likeness to the sun, had recently become the official emblem of emperors, and the luxuriant, gilt flowers on the headdress and the cord and shoulder guards assert this new authority. The bamboo fence below them, like the sacred enclosures of Shinto shrines, is a token of the strutting warrior's piety.

This opulent helmet with splayed neck guard is the one accompanying the armor on pages 82–83. According to tradition the awesome gilded copper horns replicate the blade of a garden hoe, an ancient talisman against evil spirits. Samurai sometimes tucked bits of paper bearing helpful prayers into their helmets.

IV

YOSHIMASA

THE RETREAT FROM THE WORLD

In one of the darkest hours of Japanese history, when civil war threw the country into a tumult, Japan's military ruler, Shogun Yoshimasa, spent his days composing poetry, presiding over lavish court fetes, and viewing paintings and antique porcelain. Feuding lords reduced the countryside to ashes, and the long-smoldering grievances of the peasants erupted into rioting and pillage. Meanwhile the shogun meditated in his gardens and designed new palaces. It would be difficult to imagine an era of more startling contrasts than the period from the mid-fourteenth through the sixteenth century, when the Ashikaga family held the shogunate. The period is known as the Muromachi, after the district in Kyōto where the Ashikaga leader resided. Two Ashikaga shoguns, Yoshimitsu, who lived from 1358 to 1408, and his grandson Yoshimasa, 1436 to 1490—both great connoisseurs—brought about a renaissance of Japanese arts. But their preoccupation with art, philosophy, and literature, and their unbridled spending on palaces, gardens, paintings, and ceramics led to a political collapse.

The shogun Ashikaga Yoshimasa, in court dress in this fifteenth-century portrait, was a weak ruler but presided over the brilliant renaissance of the Muromachi period.

The turmoil of the Muromachi period had its roots in the triumph over the Mongols. All Japan had formed a united front to repel the Mongol invasions; but that spirit of unity disintegrated in the decades following the victory as the warrior's code of loyalty collided with the warrior's right to spoils. Traditionally the emperor or shogun rewarded his generals and soldiers with grants of land, seized from the defeated armies. Since the Mongols had been a foreign enemy, there were no lands to hand out to the victors. Soldiers from all over Japan wrote petitions to the shogun, expressing their anger that this custom was not being honored. One samurai wrote, "During the Mongol attack I . . . boarded an enemy vessel and, though wounded, took one prisoner. Later, in the attack on Takashima I took two prisoners. . . . Though a reward was recommended, I have been left out of the general recognition of merit, and my grief is extreme. . . . Mere bystanders have put in claims and been rewarded. . . . Why should I, who was wounded, have to wait empty?"

Disgruntled warrior-chiefs battled one another, and the ties between samurai and shogun weakened, so the emperor Go-Daigo believed the time was right to throw off the yoke of the shogun. He found allies among the disaffected chiefs, who ousted the shogun and burned Kamakura. Go-Daigo then made the same mistake that had brought down the shogun: he failed to recompense his generals. The leader of the Ashikaga, Takauji, simply took over the lands of the shogun as his war prize, in defiance of the emperor. Go-Daigo sent armies against him, but Takauji captured Kyōto, put the emperor to flight, and enthroned a rival emperor who named him shogun. Thus from 1336 Japan had two emperors: the Ashikaga puppet reigned in Kyōto while Go-Daigo and his successors ruled in the south. Both emperors had powerful supporters who battled incessantly until 1392, when Shogun Yoshimitsu proposed a compromise—the southern emperor could return to Kyōto, and the two rival branches of the imperial family would alternate on the throne. The compromise was a trick. Once the imperial regalia were returned to Kyōto, Yoshimitsu forbade the southern line from occupying the throne.

Yoshimitsu reversed a long-standing policy of the shogunate, one

Three samurai in elegant robes eat rice from lacquer bowls, while a woman prepares to serve them sake, or rice wine, in this fourteenth-century scroll. Despite savage clan wars, samurai under the Ashikaga shoguns eagerly embraced such genteel amenities, which flourished in the court at Kyōto.

that Shogun Yoritomo had regarded as essential to the preservation of military rule. Yoritomo and his successors had kept their generals away from Kyōto, where they might have succumbed to the blandishments of easy court life. Yoshimitsu, in order to keep a close eye on his vassals, encouraged them to stay at Kyōto, tempted them with lavish ceremonials and fetes, and conducted all important business through a tangled bureaucracy of courtiers.

The rough soldiers of the Ashikaga who flocked to Kyōto provoked hilarity among the aristocratic courtiers whose families went back to the Heian period. They referred to the soldiers as the "sudden lords," arrayed in costly garments that did not sit well on their muscular frames, handling delicate ceramics in their calloused hands, and generally putting on the airs of urban dandies. But under the tutelage of Yoshimitsu, and later, Yoshimasa, the warrior-chiefs acquired more than just cultural polish. They patronized the finest artists, learned the intricacies of art criticism, and provided the wealth that supported the Muromachi revival of the arts.

Yoshimitsu's policy of promoting the arts had a deeper, political purpose. The shogun was not content to rule by military might alone: he wanted to be regarded as a legitimate ruler. Yoshimitsu believed that he could achieve this legitimacy by making himself the cultural leader of Japan. Pomp and glamor were important to Yoshimitsu's policy, because he knew the necessity of keeping the court entertained. But he also had faith in the higher value and power of art to alter ways of seeing and thinking and to provide a path to enlightenment. Yoshimitsu's artistic ideals derived from the shogun's devotion to Zen Buddhism.

The Zen sect of Buddhism became the virtual state religion during the Muromachi period. Zen taught that long study of Buddhist scriptures was not necessary for attaining enlightenment. Indeed, logical analysis blocked enlightenment, which should come suddenly, "like the flash of a sword," in the words of one writer. The means to enlightenment was self-discipline through arduous meditation. The spirit of Zen pervaded the arts of the Muromachi period, and, in fact, many artists of that time were Zen priests.

In this sixteenth-century ink painting, three high-ranking officials dressed as carefree hermits revel in a forest grove. Retreat to the wilderness was a popular practice inspired by the spread of Zen Buddhism during the Muromachi period.

The influence of Zen was most apparent in painting and architecture. In both of these arts, Zen inspired extremely simple styles, with details stripped away, because spare works promoted meditation. Japanese landscape artists, who had studied in China and mastered the techniques of the landscapists of the Sung dynasty, created tranquil landscapes with ink alone. They believed that colors could portray only the surface of a landscape, not its essence. Zen masters designed buildings, set among rigidly stylized gardens (see pages 96–109), with meditation as a prime purpose. The top story of the Kinkaku-ji, or "Golden Pavilion," built in 1397 for Yoshimitsu's retirement, held a simple, small room with a ceiling of gold leaf, where the shogun, by then a Zen monk, could meditate.

Yoshimasa, Yoshimitsu's grandson, succeeded to the shogunate in 1449 after his father, Yoshinori, had been assassinated by a vassal who feared his lands were going to be taken away by the shogun. Yoshimasa had little inclination to rule; he was much more concerned with painting, reading, erecting palaces, and drinking tea. Zen monks, who found that tea could keep them awake for long periods of meditation, developed a tea ceremony in which a group of friends came together in a simply furnished room to drink according to a strictly prescribed Zen ritual and discuss the aesthetics of a painting they had brought or a poem one of them had recited. Disciplined concentration on the ritual of brewing and drinking the tea freed the mind from worldly cares. Yoshimasa transformed this austere rite into a large-scale display of costly antique tea bowls, specially collected for the shogun's ceremonies. At any rate Yoshimasa required no special discipline to free his mind of the cares of office.

Yoshimasa's lack of interest in government contributed to the precipitous decline in the power of the shogunate. Once again the provincial landlords had gained a great deal of independence because of the weakness of the central government. Yoshimasa allowed his court ladies to exercise the little power remaining to the shogun. Any government edict could be vetoed by Yoshimasa's wife, his mother, or one of his mistresses. Without giving any thought to

THE FLASH
OF TRUTH

The most influential school of thought among the Ashikaga shoguns and their regents was Zen, a sect of Buddhism that reached Japan from China in feudal times. Zen had no canon and no prescribed rituals. Instead its practitioners believed in satori—a flash of truth attained through intense concentration. The founder of this mystical sect was an Indian holy man named Bodhidharma. According to legend he arrived in China in A.D. 520 and stopped to visit the emperor Wu, a devout Buddhist who tried to impress his guest by boasting of the many temples he had built. Dismayed at his vanity, Bodhidharma left the palace, crossed the Yangtze River on a reed, then traveled until he reached a mountain monastery. There he sat facing a cliff, meditating for so long—reportedly nine years—that his legs fell off.

This mythical ordeal dramatized the severe self-discipline that formed the basis of Zen, which required its adherents to meditate on seemingly irrational problems, called koans, intended to undermine the rational side of the mind. (The most famous of these philosophical riddles asks, "What is the sound of one hand clapping?") Like the Buddha, Bodhidharma—whom the Japanese called Daruma—attracted many followers who passed his teachings on. Eventually the way of Zen touched most of Japanese life, and even children unwittingly paid homage to it with a favorite toy known as Daruma—a round doll that is legless.

A thirteenth-century portrayal of Daruma, first patriarch of Zen Buddhism, captures the sage's sternness and legendary powers of concentration.

where the money would come from, the shogun began to build a new palace for himself and another palace for his mother. When funds ran low he borrowed from Zen Buddhist temples.

The Zen priests who lent money to the shogun had amassed great fortunes from trade with the Chinese. The priests—the only people in Japan who could speak idiomatic as well as archaic Chinese—made regular trading voyages to the mainland. The Chinese bought Japanese raw materials, such as copper and sulphur, and decorative objects, such as fans and lacquered pieces. But most of all the Chinese were eager to acquire Japanese swords, the best in the world. In one year the Chinese bought thirty-seven thousand Japanese swords. In return the Zen priests brought home Sung landscapes, ceramics, books, textiles, and vast amounts of cash, in the form of copper coins. So lucrative was this trade for the Japanese that early in the fifteenth century there was a coin shortage in China: all the Chinese money was in Japan.

When borrowing money proved insufficient for his building projects, Yoshimasa resorted to harsher and harsher taxation. His tax collectors extracted as much as seventy percent of the farmers' produce in taxes. In the cities the tax collectors resorted to numerous levies to raise funds for their lords—a house tax, a rice-shop tax, a sake tax, and a cart tax, to name a few. Farmers carrying their produce to the cities and merchants transporting goods across the countryside had to contend with another tax system—the road tolls. Every landowner, official, and temple administrator erected barriers along the roads that passed through his property or jurisdiction. Travelers had to pay a toll and a cargo assessment in order to proceed. On some roads there was a barrier every mile.

After paying all their taxes and road tolls, farmers often had no cash left to buy seeds for the next season's planting and were forced to borrow money from pawnbrokers. Poor samurai who had mortgaged their small holdings also found themselves in financial straits. Threatened with the loss of their lands and goods, the peasants and samurai sought relief from the shogun, who issued Edicts of Good Government that would erase the debts.

The Muromachi passion for refinement and for things Chinese inspired this folding screen in which a group of gentlemen appreciate what were known as the four scholarly accomplishments: chess, lute playing, calligraphy, and painting. Imported from China, these activities flowered under Yoshimasa.

The first Edicts of Good Government, issued by the Kamakura regime, had been intended only for the samurai. During Yoshimasa's reign the peasants demanded equal treatment. They rioted in the countryside and in Kyōto, attacking the shops of pawnbrokers and other moneylenders to destroy the loan records and retrieve the valuables they had pawned. Shaken by the violence of the recurring riots, Yoshimasa issued a stream of thirteen edicts, usually allowing the debtors to reclaim their goods and lands on payment of just ten percent of the debt.

The financial ruse of the edict, which turned the private economy into a chaotic mess, could do little to lessen the miseries suffered by the peasants during the famines and plagues that struck Japan from 1457 through 1461. The sick and starving flocked to the capital in the vain hope of getting just a tidbit of the fabulous wealth on display there. A Buddhist monk set up a city of grass huts near Kyōto where eighty thousand refugees were housed. At one time twelve hundred bodies were found in the city's rivers. Yoshimasa ignored the appalling misery all around him. The emperor Go-Hanazono, who was touched by the plight of his people but was without the means to help them, resorted to a traditional Japanese technique of getting attention: he addressed a poem to the shogun.

> The suffering people struggle for ferns on Mount Shouyang
> While everywhere their ovens are banked, and
>   their bamboo doors shut.
> It is spring and the second month; yet there is no joy in verse.
> For whom are the colors of the land bursting forth?

The answer to the final line was Shogun Yoshimasa, who was no doubt planning his spring trips to the country to view the flowers and picnic among courtiers with their chopsticks of gold.

Yoshimasa grew tired of even the light duties of a figurehead and in 1464, when he was twenty-nine, announced his intention to relinquish the shogunate to his brother and retire. His wife, Tomi-ko, was opposed to the idea because she wanted her son to succeed to the

A robed scholar, standing at left in this Chinese-style hanging scroll, listens respectfully to a Zen priest seated at a table, on which is a simple flower arrangement. The art of arranging flowers was regarded as a natural expression of Zen; even warriors practiced it to achieve composure.

shogunate. Tomi-ko and Yoshimasa's brother both enlisted the aid of great country lords, called daimyos, with large armies at their command. Soon two rival hosts, of eighty thousand men each, were encamped outside Kyōto. The succession dispute provided a convenient pretext for the daimyos, who had grown rich from commerce and farming, to settle their private scores. In 1467 the armies outside Kyōto clashed, signaling the start of an eleven-year period of sporadic fighting known as the Onin War. It was no chivalrous contest of samurai, but a brutal slaughter fought by masses of troops.

Ironically the man who touched off the conflict, Shogun Yoshimasa, came through it unscathed, not because the daimyos held him in any honor, but because he was irrelevant. The Onin War ended in victory for no one, with the possible exception of Tomi-ko, who lent money to the combatants at a huge profit. No daimyo emerged triumphant, but the tottering rule of the shogunate collapsed. The upheavals of the Muromachi period also reduced the imperial family to near poverty. The emperors had become insignificant even as figureheads. The shogun and the daimyos displayed cold indifference toward the degradation the emperors had to endure. In 1500 one emperor lay unburied for six weeks because there was no money for a funeral. Another emperor supported himself by selling his calligraphy—anyone could come to the palace and pay the emperor to copy a favorite literary passage.

With the country in ruins, Yoshimasa turned his thoughts to building his retirement villa. On the grounds of an estate outside Kyōto, Yoshimasa constructed the Ginkaku-ji, or "Silver Pavilion" (see page 95), named for the silver-leaf decoration Yoshimasa intended to apply to the interior, but never did. The two-story pavilion is a simple, almost subdued building with an exterior of unpainted wood, overlooking a lake and set amid tranquil gardens. On this estate Yoshimasa spent his final years meditating, examining his collection of Chinese ceramics and paintings, and drinking tea with his coteries, as the daimyos once again went to war. Yoshimasa died in 1490 as he had lived—in the quiet, luxurious eye of a turbulent political storm that touched him not at all.

EARTHLY
PARADISES

*Yoshimasa's villa, the two-storied Silver Pavilion, stands
before a magnificent garden pond, the centerpiece of an
estate built for the shogun about 1483.*

While all of the arts shone in the Muromachi age, the most conspicuous treasures were the gardens in and around the capital of Kyōto. Usually combined with architecture, these man-made landscapes fed an intense enjoyment of nature that was one of the profoundest traits in the Japanese character. It had its roots in religion, for many of the ancient Shintō gods were nature spirits venerated in rocks and hills and trees. And the awesome beauty of Japan itself also fostered this kinship with nature. The art of creating a garden came to Japan from China in the seventh century, and in typical fashion the Japanese imbued gardens with a taste and feeling all their own. The gardens of Muromachi owed much to landscape painting, and many were conceived by famous painters, who translated to nature the effects they achieved with ink and brush on paper. The other great influence on garden art was Zen Buddhism: its precepts of restraint and austerity resulted in artfully compressed, symbolic versions of nature intended to promote meditation as much as aesthetic pleasure.

Artists varied their gardens by size and by the choice and placement of water, stones, moss, and other raw materials. Water shimmering in ponds and pools is the heart of the garden, here and on pages 98–99, that surrounds Yoshimasa's Silver Pavilion. Probably planned by Soami, one of the finest Muromachi painters, the garden was laid out for strolling. But it also formed an exquisite picture when viewed from the balcony of the shogun's mansion.

A quiet pond in the garden of the Silver Pavilion reflects the image of a six-foot-high cone of white sand, whose truncated shape suggests a volcano. The gleaming structure was probably only a small pile of sand in Yoshimasa's day, and successive nobles tending the garden added to it.

Water swirls around a large stone in these two views, from different angles, of a cascade pool that is part of the original design in the Silver Pavilion garden. Garden artists took extraordinary care in placing stones, seeking arrangements that were not only natural and lovely, but that evoked a mood; here the stone suggests solitary resistance against the water's ceaseless flow. Yoshimasa especially loved his garden bathed in moonlight. The pool is called Senget-sugen—"Moon Washing Spring"—presumably because the moon's image, dancing on the surface, looks as though it is being washed by the water.

Moss, rather than water, dominates the luxuriant garden, here and on the next four pages, that blankets the grounds of a Zen monastery in western Kyōto called Saiho-ji. Originally built in the twelfth century, the garden was reconstructed in 1339 by Soseki, a renowned priest-gardener who made it one of the first stroll gardens in Japan. Earlier gardens had been designed for viewing only from a building or from an excursion boat floating on a pond. But at Saiho-ji, monks as well as pleasure-seekers could wander through verdant glens that melted into one another like the panels of a great folding screen. The monastery's sheltered position and rich soil encouraged a profusion of mosses, and over the years nature has produced more than forty varieties that fan out in undulating waves of different shades and textures.

The garden entranced aristocrats and military leaders alike, but no one more than Yoshimasa. Gaining inspiration for his own garden at the Silver Pavilion, the shogun visited Saiho-ji several times a year and concluded, "The beauty of this garden never diminishes!"

In a forested patch of the moss garden at Saiho-ji, several species of moss cover the ground with a velvety carpet, while gray-green lichens create a sensuous down on the tree trunks. Trees were often sent as gifts from one temple to another.

A thick cloak of moss flows over the weathered root of a tree, evoking a mood of great tranquillity that the Japanese call yūgen,

which means "mysterious beauty." So lush did Saiho-ji become that legends arose claiming it was the home of beneficent spirits.

OVERLEAF: *Two stones float in a sea of star-shaped moss. The Japanese endowed stones with gender, and garden artists would emphasize this by placing a tall, straight male stone (at right) next to a flatter stone, which was considered feminine.*

The garden at Daisen-in (at left and on pages 108–109), a small temple within another large Zen monastery, Daitoku-ji, has no water and practically no vegetation. Utterly spare, like a painting executed with a few masterful strokes, it is one of the finest examples of *kare sansui*, or dry landscape gardening. Within the space of a few hundred square feet, the artist arranged rocks, gravel, and a few shrubs to create not only an illusion of nature but of a vast panorama. Tradition attributes the design to Soami, the great painter and landscapist from Yoshimasa's court; however, it may also have been the work of Kogaku, the priest who founded the temple about 1513, as the Muromachi age was drawing to an end. The sole purpose of this garden was to encourage contemplation. But the way that it distills the world, so purely and beautifully, places it at the apex of the art of gardening.

An austere landscape of rocks and gravel surrounds the abbot's quarters (lower left) at Daisen-in temple. Tall, rugged stones (upper left and center) represent mountains, out of which pours an imaginary waterfall that widens into a river of white gravel raked into wavy patterns. The fictive water races under a stone bridge, then along a veranda, where it encounters a series of rock arrangements.

Three rocks rise like islands from the riverbed, above, as it courses past the veranda, where screens hang in front of a study that is decorated within by Soami's paintings. The stones at Daisen-in are remarkably varied, and may have been culled from the Ashikaga shoguns' estates, which were falling into ruin when work began on this garden. The riverbed curves under the veranda and seems to head toward another area where a conical heap of sand, opposite, appears in the midst of a sandy plain. This carefully raked expanse symbolizes the ocean—and hence the viewer, walking around the veranda, would trace the river's journey from beginning to end.

V

HIDEYOSHI'S MIGHTY REGENCY

THE EVANESCENCE OF POWER

When I was about to enter my dear mother's womb, she had an auspicious dream. That night, the sunlight filled her room so that it was like noontime inside it. All were overwhelmed with astonishment...and the diviner proclaimed: 'This is a wondrous sign that when the child reaches his prime...he will radiate his glory to the ten thousand directions.'"

The child indeed fulfilled the diviner's prophecy. He was Toyotomi Hideyoshi, who grew up to become one of Japan's greatest generals and the ruler who imposed a lasting unity on his country. He may also have been the wealthiest man in the history of Japan up to that time. Hideyoshi owned gold and silver mines. He built an immense castle, eight miles in circumference; entertained the emperor at his Mansion of Assembled Pleasures; filled a street with trays of gold and silver coins—and gave them away. A Japanese writer who probably witnessed Hideyoshi's fabled extravagances exclaimed that he was "a river, an ocean of magnanimity, and strove for magnificence in all things."

In this formally posed portrait of Toyotomi Hideyoshi only his thrusting head and inquisitive eyes betray the bold personality of the man who unified Japan.

The story of Hideyoshi's conception, which he wrote down when he was in his fifties, reveals a great deal about his character. In the first place Hideyoshi actually believed the story of the miraculous light, which he took to be a sign that he was a man apart, that he had "met Heaven's Will." The story is also revealing in what it leaves out: there is no mention of a father. Hideyoshi may have been the son of a peasant or of a low-level courtier—a "flunky," as some contemporary historians speculated. In either case his origins were humble, so Hideyoshi kept his past a secret, preferring to let legend take the place of truth. So successful was he at hiding his origins that the place of Hideyoshi's birth is unknown, and the year of his birth is uncertain—either 1536 or 1537.

Hideyoshi was born in an era of upheaval that the Japanese called Sengoku Jidai—the "Period of the Warring States." The Ashikaga shoguns clung to office, but were powerless. The feudal lords had begun to battle one another almost as soon as the Onin War had ended, and Buddhist temples also fielded armies to wrest what land they could from the lords. The Onin War had erased all vestiges of chivalry from combat, which was also transformed by the profusion of fortresses built by country lords to guard their domains. The Period of the Warring States lasted roughly a century; the fighting might have been even more protracted but for a storm that drove a Chinese vessel onto Japan's shore in 1542.

The ship was carrying three Portuguese traders. In 1498 the Portuguese navigator Vasco da Gama had rounded the southern tip of Africa, sailed north to India, and opened a sea route between Asia and Europe. In just four decades the Portuguese established a string of trading stations from Africa to China, loading their ships with Asian spices for the eager markets of Europe. The Japanese who happened upon the grounded vessel, on the small island of Tanegashima off the southern coast of Kyūshū, were the first to look upon Europeans. Someone aboard the vessel was able to communicate with the Japanese by scratching Chinese characters into the sand. The Portuguese, practiced in the art of impressing potential customers, gave a demonstration of their muskets. The son of one of the

Riding in a palanquin to a cherry blossom viewing festival, Hideyoshi, at right, is surrounded by his supporters. One fashionable man, center, wears the high-crowned hat, jacket, and pantaloons copied from recently arrived Portuguese traders.

Japanese who was present wrote an account of the scene: "It [a musket] was about two or three feet long, straight, heavy and hollow. One end was closed and near this end was a small hole through which fire was to be lighted. Some mysterious powder was put into it with a small round piece of lead, and when one lit the powder through that hole the lead piece was discharged and hit everything. Light like lightning was seen, and noise like thunder heard; bystanders closed their ears with their hands and flying birds and running beasts fell before them." The Japanese quickly recovered from their initial shock and took shooting lessons from the Portuguese. Soon they were hitting targets at a hundred paces.

The accidental landfall brought more Portuguese traders to the new land, where the Japanese welcomed the Europeans warmly. With the traders came Jesuit missionaries, who won the respect of the upper classes by their scientific knowledge and their discipline—which contrasted sharply with the decadence of the warlike Buddhist priests. The Japanese had not yet heard, for example, about the voyage of Columbus. Large numbers of Japanese converted to Christianity, roughly 150,000 over the next 40 years. But the most immediate impact of the European arrival was wrought by the musket. The Japanese not only bought muskets from the Portuguese, they rapidly learned to make their own, as well as gunpowder and even cannons.

Among the first Japanese to realize that the musket had revolutionized warfare were Hideyoshi and his commander, Oda Nobunaga. Nobunaga was a minor chieftain who won great military success by his resourcefulness. He won his first battle, in 1560, against an army of twenty-five thousand with only three thousand troops of his own, in a surprise attack during a rainstorm. In a battle against a cavalry force, he covered the battlefield with stockades and placed musketeers behind them. He organized his musketeers into three groups, two of which loaded their weapons while the other fired at the charging horsemen. The steady fire from the cover of the stockades routed the enemy.

Hideyoshi began as a junior officer in Nobunaga's army, but rose through the ranks when Nobunaga noticed his skill at reducing fortresses. On one occasion Hideyoshi had ordered his men to divert a river and flood the enemy's defenses. Hideyoshi was a high-ranking officer by 1568, when Nobunaga entered Kyoto in triumph to be named deputy shogun. For the next fourteen years Nobunaga and Hideyoshi fought together to subdue enemy clans and the Ikkō-shū, or "single-minded," sect of warrior Buddhist priests. In 1582 Nobunaga was assassinated by one of his own generals or one of his general's men, whom Hideyoshi later killed. Following Nobunaga's death his officers recognized Hideyoshi as their leader. After ten more years of fighting, Hideyoshi was master of Japan. The only lord strong enough to challenge him, Tokugawa Ieyasu, had had his fill of bloodshed and made peace with Hideyoshi in exchange for some independence in his own lands. In 1585 and 1586 the emperor conferred on Hideyoshi the titles of regent and chancellor. The regency was traditionally occupied by a member of the Fujiwara family—a technicality Hideyoshi satisfied by persuading a Fujiwara to adopt him.

Hideyoshi the ruler was, if anything, more daring, resourceful, and insistent upon discipline than Hideyoshi the general. In 1583 he ordered a survey of all the farms in Japan to find out what their exact size and yields were. Hideyoshi later swept away the tangle of absentee landlords and gave the fields to the farmers themselves—a move that was not entirely altruistic. Hideyoshi planned to establish a permanent class of peasants by law. Indeed Hideyoshi announced his grand design for Japanese society in edicts of 1585 and 1586. In effect he was trying to freeze society—he forbade anyone to leave the service of his employer without permission and specifically ordered samurai to stay under their current chiefs. Farmers were ordered to remain farmers. No one who did not already live in a town could move into one. Landless men, particularly wandering samurai, were to be reported to the government.

Other military men before Hideyoshi had created new governments, imposed their will on the people, and even made the emperors their puppets; but none had possessed Hideyoshi's absolute

A stable for their horses nearby, samurai gather at one of the temporary tea huts erected for Hideyoshi's last, extravagant reception. A few months before his death the regent invited military comrades to come and talk over old times.

power and virtually inexhaustable wealth. In Emperor Shōmu's time the discovery of a gold lode had been so rare an event that it was considered a miracle. Many new gold and silver mines were found during Hideyoshi's reign because he ordered increased prospecting. The mines of the nation served as Hideyoshi's personal bank—every gold and silver mine sent him a portion of its yield, and several mines were entirely his.

Previous rulers had displayed their wealth with a degree of decorum. The taste of even the profligate shogun Yoshimasa was called "astringent" by the Japanese. Hideyoshi delighted in his wealth and never ceased to find imaginative ways to proclaim it. He also understood the political uses of display. Hideyoshi generously underwrote the restoration of the Imperial Palaces at Kyōto, but constructed for himself the Mansion of Assembled Pleasures, a vastly more lavish Kyōto residence, with a roof covered in gold. In the compound of the mansion, in 1589, Hideyoshi ordered an avenue filled with trays of gold coins—three hundred yards of trays, over sixteen thousand pounds of gold. There Hideyoshi tantalized an assembly of vassals and nobles, including the emperor's brother. As an official read from a list of recipients—who came mostly from Hideyoshi's own family—the trays were handed out until the glittering avenue was bare. The tea ceremonies, traditionally a ritual of Zen austerity, became for Hideyoshi yet another means of ostentation—even in his fashionably rustic tea hut, where only clay vessels were used. For elaborate palace teas, Hideyoshi commissioned a tearoom entirely covered with gold leaf.

As the crowning symbol of his might and wealth, Hideyoshi built a castle at Osaka that was among the largest structures in the world. Work had begun on the castle in 1583. Impatient to see the castle finished, Hideyoshi set tens of thousands of men to work on it and threatened their overseers with exile if the project lagged behind schedule. Every day a fleet of ships arrived with stones for the towers (of which there were over 125 in number) and for the double circuit of walls that enclosed 187 acres of land. The centerpiece of the castle—indeed of the whole nation, for Hideyoshi made the fortress

TEXT CONTINUED ON PAGE 122

Hideyoshi's tea hut, orginally at Fushimi Castle, had a rustic, but highly stylish, thatch.

PRICELESS POVERTY

For the several centuries since its introduction from China, tea drinking had generated ritual and veneration. In the sixteenth century sundry tea traditions combined to become a distinctively Japanese institution: the poverty tea ceremony, ruled by tea masters who were connoisseurs of tea delectation and of the arts.

Masters such as Sen no Rikyū, adviser to the regent Hideyoshi, set a style of mock poverty that tea men eagerly followed. In a garden of contrived naturalness, the merchant, lord, or imperial official erected a tea hut resembling a simple country cottage, furnished with a few utensils, flowers, and a calligraphic scroll. To this idealized haven from worldliness the rich man invited either friends or reconcilable enemies, seated them on straw mats, and served them with his own hand. Communal humility and appreciation of the exquisitely minimal setting would chasten and refresh the souls of the tea drinkers.

Meditative calm was but one face of the proceedings, however, for tea men also schemed feverishly to outdo one another in aesthetic simplicity. An innovative detail of hut or garden, a collection of superior vessels gave a man cachet. Tea masters, the final arbiters of value, were not above playing games. Allegedly in time the august Rikyū lost Hideyoshi's favor for secret profiteering in tea bowls, caddies, kettles, and jars.

The interior of the Fushimi tea hut, opposite, reveals emphatic use of raw woods and a modular plan based on the shapes of its straw floor mats, called tatami. The plaque reads: Place of Idleness.

The freshwater jar was the largest and most conspicuous vessel in the tea ceremony. It sat in front of the host, who used it for filling his kettle and for washing the tea whisk. The ceramic jar at left, with its syrupy glazes, came from Karatsu, a region producing ordinary farm wares strongly influenced by resident Korean potters. Individual vessels were celebrated not only for their physical qualities but also simply because a certain tea master had selected them. While he designed and commissioned certain pieces, the master's acumen enabled him to discover others embodying his aesthetic ideal among the everyday containers or the antiquities of the wealthy collector. Once objects were so chosen they were imbued with personalities, given descriptive names, and bought and sold at monstrous prices.

Having kindled a charcoal fire in the brazier or sunken hearth, the tea ceremony host put his kettle on to boil. But things were seldom as spontaneous as they seemed. He watched the water closely through classically prescribed stages of bubbling, then dipped it out at the most propitious moment. An apparently battered cast-iron kettle, such as the one at right favored by Rikyū, had come by its soft look through intricate foundry processes of reheating, dimpling with a pointed tool, and washing with plum vinegar and lacquer. The craftsman who made such tea objects might be honored with the extravagant title of "foremost in the world."

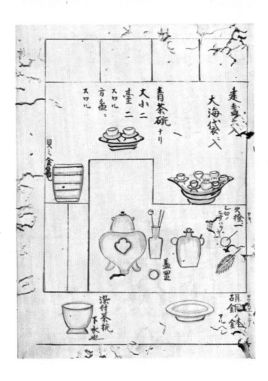

The immaculately arranged objects in this diagram include a heart-shaped brazier with a kettle on top, a Chinese-style tea leaf storage jar with handles, a feather for hearth sweeping, food dishes, and water jars. All were used for a palace tea, a type of tea party predating and differing from the poverty cere-mony. The palace tea host gave his guests the sensual pleasure of elegant furnishings, food, and drink rather than an opportunity to be ascetic. Enthusiasts of the tea cults wrote tea party diaries and treatises, and the page here is from a record book kept for a fifteenth-century Ashikaga shogun. It tells how tea vessels might be properly displayed and critically rates a long list of Chinese paintings, for palace teas were occasions of unmitigated pomp, and Chinese art objects connoted power. The palace tradition persisted even as the Ashikaga shogunate vanished. In addition to his poverty hut, Hideyoshi had a palace tearoom lined and fitted out in gold.

"Spear Sheath," the tea caddy at right, belonged to Hideyoshi and is considered the finest ever made in Japan. It came from a kiln probably founded by a potter trained in China, and has the tactile appeal loved by poverty tea men. Below, beside its storage box, lies a thin, bamboo tea scoop carved by Rikyū. Slight as it is, the scoop was the most expressive of a master's tools. Scooping powdered green tea from the caddy into a bowl and adding a portion of hot water, the master beat the mixture to a froth with his bamboo whisk and then served it.

TSUTSUIZUTSU

HAKU-TEMMOKU

Because it passed from hand to hand, the tea bowl embodied the sharing aspect of a ceremony. The bowls here represent several popular types, and each was either owned or praised by Rikyū or Hideyoshi. Working under Rikyū's direction, master potter Chōjirō developed the famous raku glaze technique and hand-formed the bowls called Ichimonji (below), Muichibutsu (opposite, top), and Shunkan (opposite, bottom). Their irregular shapes, grainy

ICHIMONJI

MUICHIBUTSU

textures, and soft density of color evoke the "worship of the imperfect" intrinsic to poverty tea. The same aesthetic commended Tsutsuizutsu (opposite, top), with its crackled, fissured glaze and utilitarian design. Its earthy warmth of color especially qualified it for use in a thatched tea hut. By contrast the haku-temmoku bowl (opposite, center), and yuteki-temmoku (right), with lustrous glazes, suited the formality of a palace tea.

YUTEKI-TEMMOKU

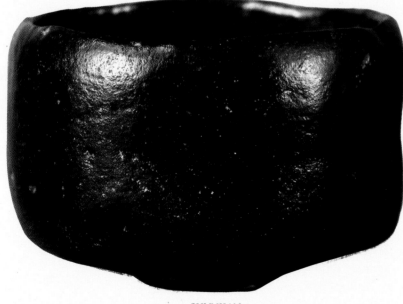

SHUNKAN

TEXT CONTINUED FROM PAGE 115

the seat of his government—was an eight-story tower, over one hundred feet high, clad in blue and gold. It shone over land and sea like a beacon of his sovereignty.

The overpowering scale of the castle was echoed in the furnishings within. In a sense Hideyoshi brought the world into his domain of stone: he commissioned the finest painters to fill the walls with painted skies, forests, gardens, and other landscapes, through which mythical animals prowled. The walls could not hold enough art for Hideyoshi; he ordered in addition one hundred painted screens for the castle's rooms. Virtually everything he would have to touch he ordered in gold—his bowls, his chopsticks, the locks on the doors, the latches on the windows. Nothing was exempt from his passion for display. A visitor lamented, "the very privies are decorated with gold and silver, and paintings in fine colors. All these precious things are used as if they were dirt. Ah! Ah!"

Hideyoshi personally led a group of Portuguese Jesuits on a tour of the castle in 1586. Accompanied by a woman carrying the keys to the maze of passageways and rooms, Hideyoshi threw open doors and windows to display his treasures. Hideyoshi was beside himself with pride. One of the Jesuits who was there, Luis Frois, wrote that Hideyoshi exclaimed, "This room you see here is full of gold, this one of silver; this other compartment is full of bales of silk and damask, that one with robes. . . ." Hideyoshi showed the priests his armory and took them up to the top of the golden tower where the ruler pointed out the thousands of men toiling below on the plain. He also ushered the guests into his private chambers where they were astonished to see, decorated in the by-then-expected gold trimmings, two European-style beds, probably the only ones in Japan. The Japanese slept on mats, and Hideyoshi probably endured many sleepless nights for the sake of owning the ultimate in exotica.

The impression of Hideyoshi that Father Frois carried away was one of "superb arrogance." Hideyoshi had cloaked the shame of his low birth with gold and impregnable pride. At a reception for Spanish envoys from the colony on the Philippines, Hideyoshi spontaneously burst out, "When I was born, a sunbeam fell on my

Townsmen and samurai celebrating a July festival trundle red-draped floats—one like a ship—through Kyōto streets. The old, wooden city sprang to new life under a flourishing merchant class whose festive spirit kept pace with that of the imperial circle.

chest." He boasted that no emperor had ever ruled a united Japan, "and I have subdued all of it."

Hideyoshi so deeply believed in his own magnificence that he could not see when it had become the butt of a joke. A Spanish ambassador brought a trained elephant to Osaka as a gift. Hideyoshi emerged from the castle, holding his six-year-old son by the hand. As the ruler approached the elephant, its keeper prodded the animal to kneel down and trumpet—a standard routine, but one that enthralled Hideyoshi when the envoy told him, tongue in cheek, that the elephant had recognized his majesty and therefore was kneeling in obeisance.

His own courtiers dared not trifle with Hideyoshi. In 1589 Hideyoshi's aged tea master and confidant, Sen no Rikyū, donated money to build a gate at a Zen Buddhist temple. In gratitude the monks placed a statue of Rikyū near the top of the gate. One day when Hideyoshi walked under the gate he looked up and saw the statue of Rikyū towering above him. He took it as a deliberate insult and ordered the statue destroyed. In 1591, perhaps because of political intrigues or because of an argument over selling tea utensils, Hideyoshi ordered his old friend to commit ritual suicide.

A barbaric episode near the end of Hideyoshi's life lends weight to the theory that he was, at times, deranged. Hideyoshi profoundly desired to start a dynasty, but his firstborn son died in 1590. Having no other heir at the time, Hideyoshi appointed his nephew Hidetsugu as regent, to ensure an orderly succession in case of his sudden death. But Hidetsugu proved to be a cruel and despotic ruler, the "murdering regent," as the people called him.

In 1593 one of Hideyoshi's concubines gave birth to a second son, Hideyori, thus reopening the question of the succession in Hideyoshi's mind. He ordered Hidetsugu to commit suicide and then commanded that the dead man's children—Hideyori's potential rivals—be stabbed to death along with thirty entirely innocent women attendants. The body of Hidetsugu's heir was buried below those of the women in a mass grave, which was covered up with a heap of earth.

A popular if willful regent, Hideyoshi enlarged his fame by commissioning plays about himself and paintings of his public appearances. His hand lifted in salutation, he is accompanied here by a lady in yellow robes and a long-haired boy bearing a sword—probably his wife and Hideyori, his son.

Whether it was madness or simple ambition that finally impelled Hideyoshi on his last military adventure cannot be known; but in 1592 he launched an invasion of Korea, with thoughts of going on to China. That Hideyoshi could even consider so gargantuan a task is evidence of his unique abilities as a general and a ruler. Hideyoshi was able to equip and land in Korea a host of 150,000 men. The Japanese won easy victories against the Koreans, who were the vassals of China, and wiped out a token force of five thousand Chinese troops sent against them. But the guerrilla tactics of the Koreans and a sickness among the Japanese soldiers slowed the invasion. Worst of all the experienced Korean navy inflicted serious damage on the invasion fleet. Threatened with isolation if they lost the fleet, the Japanese generals sued for peace and withdrew. The peace agreement called for China to recognize Hideyoshi as the king of Japan—a concession Hideyoshi looked on as the fitting climax to his career. But when the Chinese envoys arrived in Kyōto for the investiture ceremony, the text of their proclamation made it clear that the Chinese emperor regarded the new king as a vassal.

Hideyoshi flew into a rage. He expelled the envoys, then sent them gifts, then dispatched messengers with a list of grievances—all in the same day, at the end of which he gave the order for a second invasion. Loyally, his generals invaded Korea again, and again they met with initial success. After defeating a strong Chinese force, the generals broke off the campaign and returned home when word reached them in 1598 that Hideyoshi had died.

Hideyoshi was laid to rest in the sanctuary of a temple, behind a gold curtain. At his death Japan was unified and wealthier than ever before. But on his deathbed, according to legend, the unifier's thoughts were not about permanence, but about the evanescence of his own life. In a final poem attributed to him, Hideyoshi wrote,

Ah! as the dew I fall,
As the dew I vanish.
Even Osaka fortress
Is a dream within a dream.

A SHADOWLESS GARDEN

At the zenith of his career Hideyoshi commissioned movable, painted paper screens that transform this temple alcove into a sun-filled woodland clearing.

Behind a cherry tree exploding with double blossoms stands a willow, its veil of new leaves trailing down. Japanese belief attributed male or

The three screens here and on the following pages, the first bearing a flowering cherry tree (above), the second a maple tree (pages 131–135), and the third a pine among the grasses (pages 136–139), adorned the walls of a memorial chapel Hideyoshi built for his firstborn son, who died at the age of two. Each screen comprises several wood-framed paper panels covered with opaque gold leaf and then dramatically painted. Brilliant colors and abundant botanical details stand out, as if in relief, against the background, expressing the Japanese adoration of nature as well as Hideyoshi's flamboyant per-

sonal tastes. The outsize scale of the panels—most of these are about five feet high and four feet wide—reflects the artistic ingenuity of the sixteenth century and one of its signal inventions: the stone-walled castle.

When he commissioned these screens, late in life, Hideyoshi had already erected five such castles, many-storied fortresses that towered over the countryside and were a sign of the progressive times. Earlier Japanese castles had been little more than fortified manor houses, low-lying wooden structures surrounded by moat or palisade. Then in 1542 guns came to Japan

female qualities to different plants and plant arrangements. Flower beds were feminine, but the flowering cherry symbolized the warrior.

and changed the conduct of war. Encircled by a maze of steep, rough stone battlements to withstand musket and cannon fire, the typical castle that Hideyoshi built satisfied both military necessity and his love of luxury. Gilt and lacquer embellished the exterior. To decorate the vast wood-beamed rooms of the inner residential quarters he summoned painters who developed screens of the type shown here. Adapting traditional modes of painting to the new challenge, they rendered out-of-door scenes realistically. Rushing waters, ancient forests, flowers, wild birds, and animals seen by the dim light from the

narrow windows seemed to come alive and restore dwellers of the barricaded castle to gentler environs. Wide expanses of gold leaf, shaped like clouds, warmed the austere rooms and made the most of slender rays of the sun.

The cherry tree, maple tree, and pine tree screens, while designed in the grand castle manner, were set apart by the genius of Hasegawa Tōhaku, a painter new to Hideyoshi's service. Tōhaku's tender regard for the smallest natural detail and his dynamic composition imbued the paintings with an optimism that must have consoled his patron for the bitter loss of his heir.

In this detail of the screen on pages 126–127, the flat abstraction of clouds, swirling water, and a spit of land contrasts with the naturalism of blossoms and branches. The gold leaf applied in blocklike rows gives the clouds the solid opacity of a stone wall.

The painter has prepared a witty surprise, for the fragility of the cherry blossoms, seen from a distance on pages 126–127, changes under close scrutiny. In fact they are plump, white medallions molded of thick chalk and glue encrusting the greenery.

Of the three screens on pages 126–139, the maple tree screen (see foldout) may best communicate the style of the painter Tōhaku and the character traits he shared with his patron. An independent artist from the north, Tōhaku began a long struggle for professional recognition after he arrived in Kyōto. By exceptional gifts and persistence he finally won the commission for these screens, prevailing over establishment rivals. He was fifty-one at the time and, like Hideyoshi, a self-made man.

Tōhaku probably intended his great maple to symbolize the heroic individual who would neither admit defeat nor be constrained by social custom—Hideyoshi himself. Rising in the center of the screen, the tree spreads across all four panels and beyond, too large to fit into the frame. The stout trunk and branches are gnarled with age but are still splendidly vital, for they have grown a fresh crown of vividly colored leaves. A variety of smaller plants and shrubs gather around the roots of the tree, flourishing under its protection, like the merchants, artisans, and lords who prospered anew under Hideyoshi's rule.

To this metaphorical portrait of a mighty but benign ruler, Tōhaku brought special skills. He had been a master of classical Japanese ink painting, which achieved its effects by the exquisite line and monochromatic shading on white paper. Colored paints on a brilliant metallic field made different demands: here his subject must have a solidity of form and bold composition that the background could not outshine.

Tōhaku met and surpassed these demands. The skills that he had learned from painting in monochrome invested his colored screens with unique subtlety. His sensitive line drawing of massive maple limbs and fragile leaves and flowers gave them equal suppleness and clarity. Additionally, by the clever variegation of color—perhaps derived from long study of shading—he made his greens, browns, and reds flow like gems set in gold.

Like Hideyoshi, who was born to poverty but grew up believing he would "radiate his glory to the ten thousand directions," Tōhaku was not cramped by his past. He modified the conventions of sixteenth-century painting to suit himself and created beauty to outlast the age.

FOLDOUT: *The Japanese worshiped well-shaped, mature trees and cultivated them with complex pruning and training techniques. Autumn excursions to gaze on the changing colors of maples were as popular as cherry blossom viewing in the spring. To show the foliage to the best advantage, gardeners often planted maple trees where the light of the setting sun would strike the branches. Though the Japanese admired the shadows that were cast by real trees, tree paintings—such as the maple tree screen on the foldout—seldom included them.* ⟶

A detail of the maple screen shows fan-shaped cockscombs, pale chrysanthemums, and—at top—a flowering shrub half hidden by cloud.

Strong asymmetry, a mark of much Japanese design, distinguishes the pine tree screen above and in detail opposite. Hibiscus plants, wiry grasses, and a slab of gold adroitly balance the ponderous volume of the tree trunk and its rigid-looking boughs. The hummocky earth has a naturalness absent in the other screens, and the prominent rocks suggest a wild mountain setting. The way an artist painted rocks, such as the crag opposite, declared the school to which he belonged and often became his hallmark.

OVERLEAF: Upright grass stalks crisscrossed by arching leaves make a passage of geometrical pattern under the larger arch of the pine tree's trunk. The black ink, here marking the pine bark's corrugations, was itself a mixture of pine soot and glue.

137

VI

THE LAST OF THE SHOGUNS

THE GILDED CAGE

A few years before his death, Hideyoshi asked the Tokugawa chief, Ieyasu, to ride out alone with him to a place overlooking Edo Bay, on the plains of the Kantō region—rich farmland near the center of the nation. There Hideyoshi silently handed his sword to Ieyasu, as a sign of his complete trust. He talked with Ieyasu about the future of Japan and, pointing his hand toward Edo Bay, said to him, "Make your capital there." On the spot he pointed out, Ieyasu built the city that later became Tōkyō.

Though Hideyoshi is often called the unifier of Japan, Ieyasu and Hideyoshi's old commander, Nobunaga, were also instrumental in consolidating the nation, each in a different way. The various methods of the three leaders were characterized in a joke that compares a disunited Japan to a songbird that will not sing. Nobunaga says, "I'll make it sing." Hideyoshi threatens, "I'll kill it if it doesn't." "I'll wait until it does sing," says Ieyasu, who finally succeeded in subduing all his enemies because he bided his time until the right moment to strike.

Tokugawa Ieyasu, looking sinister in this portrait, established his rule at Edo early in the seventeenth century, commencing the last shogunate of Japan.

Hideyoshi expected that Ieyasu would be satisfied to rule Kantō and remain loyal to Hideyoshi's son, Hideyori, but after Hideyoshi's death the daimyos divided into two factions. Some supported Hideyori, and the rest, Ieyasu. In 1600 Ieyasu defeated the armies of Hideyori's supporters at the battle of Sekigahara. Still Ieyasu did not try to depose his rival, who still had powerful backers. Instead Ieyasu made a show of loyalty to Hideyori and his family, advising him to erect a series of Buddhist shrines in memory of Hideyoshi.

In 1603 Ieyasu laid claim to the office of shogun and was granted it by the emperor; once he had secured the title, Ieyasu had no further use for the emperor and his courtiers. While he was laying his plans for the downfall of Hideyori, Ieyasu prevented any meddling by the emperor and his noble courtiers by a high-handed, but typically brilliant, stratagem. He ordered a wall to be built around "nobility town," a compound in Kyōto in which the emperor and the three hundred leading families had to reside. The shogun forbade them to leave it without permission.

To keep the pent-up emperor and nobles from conspiring against him, Ieyasu then issued five "rules of the imperial court." Prefacing rule number one with the pious statement, "Learning is the most essential of all accomplishments," he commanded the court to spend all its time studying philosophy, history, and the arts, which was tantamount to ordering them into paradise. In fact Ieyasu did have a particular paradise in mind—the past. He commissioned his finest architect, Kobori Enshū, to transform nobility town into tenth-century Kyōto, the Kyōto of *The Pillow Book* and the *Tale of Genji*. Using the natural characteristics of the open-air prison—seclusion and quiet—and adding gardens that suggested the wilderness, Enshū fashioned a world apart, where the courtiers lived happily in a dream almost literally come true.

The fantasy was heightened by the entertainments in nobility town. The courtiers frequented performances of the Nō drama—a traditional form of theater. With costumes of ethereal beauty and enigmatic masks, Nō recreated the court life of the distant past. The trappings of these dramas were more precious and inimitable than

In 1614, determined to rid himself of all opposition, Tokugawa Ieyasu stormed Osaka Castle. Here, in a detail from a seventeenth-century screen, civilians and soldiers flee across water. During the siege one of the last samurai battles in history occurred, and Ieyasu decapitated the defeated warriors.

the dramas themselves. Like the treasured possessions of Emperor Shōmu at Nara, or the calligraphic works that the Heian courtiers had delighted in, these masks and robes and the highly ritualized Nō performances belonged only to the elite of the elite. The ordinary people of Japan knew little about them.

While the imperial court was safely locked away in its world of dreams, Ieyasu engineered a confrontation with Hideyori. Casting about for a convenient excuse, Ieyasu settled upon an inscription on a temple bell. Hideyori had ordered the construction of a temple at Kyōto with a bronze statue of the Buddha and a bell. During the dedication ceremony, a messenger arrived from Ieyasu ordering the ritual halted because the inscription on the bell insulted the Tokugawa. Actually the inscription was perfectly innocuous, and Ieyasu knew it. But his bluff worked. Just as Kyōto had been thrown into chaos centuries before by an argument over the wording of an official document, the supposedly insulting inscription caused a political crisis for Hideyori. Ieyasu chose to interpret the inscription as a threat and besieged Osaka Castle in December 1614.

Hideyoshi had built Osaka Castle to be impregnable. Its walls, more than one hundred feet high, were surrounded by two moats, one of which varied in width from eighty to over a hundred yards. The castle had its own well, more than adequate food stocks, muskets for the samurai, and cannons placed on all the walls. The only problem troubling the defenders was their short supply of gunpowder, while their antagonists not only had plenty of powder but several new cannons as well.

Ieyasu opened the siege with a direct assault, which failed. Then he tried a three-day bombardment, even though he knew that the castle walls could not be brought down by cannon fire. The bombardment was intended to cause confusion and panic among the defenders and was part of Ieyasu's overall psychological strategy. Archers shot barrages of arrows into the castle compound with attached messages urging the defenders to surrender.

The particular target of Ieyasu's psychological strategy was Hideyori's mother. Ieyasu ordered his artillery officers to fire most heavily on her apartments. Eventually the strategy worked. Terrified, she pleaded with Hideyori to come to terms, and he allowed negotiations to begin. Among the envoys Hideyori sent to parley with Ieyasu was his aunt—exactly the wrong choice. He took her down to see the tunnels that miners were digging under the moat. Convinced that the fortifications were in imminent danger, Hideyori and his generals signed a peace agreement in mid-January.

By its terms Ieyasu guaranteed Hideyori's safety, provided the outer walls and moat of the castle were pulled down. Ieyasu's men then demolished the inner bastion as well as the outer. Convinced that Ieyasu was planning a second attack, Hideyori recruited more defenders and began reconstruction of the defenses, with the result that Ieyasu did renew the siege in the spring. This time the weakened castle fell. Trapped in the gold-clad tower that was the symbol of his father's might, Hideyori committed suicide, his wife was killed, and his son beheaded by Ieyasu's men.

Now Ieyasu was the undisputed master of Japan, so he conducted the affairs of the shogunate with an appropriate display of wealth. In the audience hall of his castle at Suruga, in central Honshū, Ieyasu sat on a throne covered with cloth of gold. Along the sides of the hall stretched a latticework of gold, five or six feet high, with doorways through which his attendants entered on their hands and knees in silence. The Spanish grandee who witnessed a gift-giving ceremony in this hall (and called Ieyasu emperor rather than shogun) was amazed not only at the riches on display, but also at Ieyasu's refusal to be impressed by them: "There entered one of the greatest nobles of Japan, whose high rank was evident from the gifts he brought—bars of silver and gold, silk robes and other things, all of which must have been worth more than 20,000 ducats. All this was first of all placed on some tables but I do not believe the emperor even looked at it. Then at over a hundred paces from where His Highness was seated, this [noble] prostrated himself, bowing his head so low that it looked as if he wanted to kiss the ground. Nobody said a word to him nor did he raise his eyes towards the Emperor on entering and leaving."

Even on the streets the shogun's subjects had to observe the strict

Two masked actors perform on a wooden stage erected in the garden of a shogun's palace. In the theater of the court, the audience savored the masks, elegant robes, and music as much as the setting.

protocol of keeping silent and averting their eyes when the shogun passed. In solemn processions through the streets of Edo, the only sounds heard were the rustling of harnesses and of the black silk uniforms of the shogun's guards. The Tokugawa regime was highly centralized and militaristic: it employed informers and strictly regulated the personal lives of the citizens. For example, the shoguns banned Christianity and promoted Confucian philosophy, borrowed from China, which preached submission to the state. The shoguns and daimyos kept the peasants in near poverty, and the shoguns held the daimyos' families as hostages in Edo. To buttress the regime Ieyasu and his successors closed Japan to foreigners, except the Chinese and the Dutch, who were allowed to trade out of only one port, directly regulated by the shogun.

Beginning with Ieyasu the Tokugawa banned Christianity chiefly because it was alien, but also because they feared it might undermine the rigidly fixed social hierarchy of samurai, farmer, artisan, and merchant. Under Ieyasu's son and successor, Hidetada, more than seven hundred Christians were executed, some burned alive. In 1637, under a later shogun, Christian peasants and poor samuari staged a revolt. Though their slogans were religious, their goals were political. More than twenty thousand rebels carrying portraits of saints and banners proclaiming "Praise to the Blessed Sacrament," took possession of a deserted castle near Nagasaki. The peasants and disaffected samurai nurtured the fantastic hope of ending their exploitation by the landlords and officials, who carried out a policy of "Give the peasants neither life nor death." This dictum, attributed to Ieyasu, meant that the shoguns would allow the peasants to subsist, but barely. Under orders from the shogun, the daimyos around Nagasaki hurled an army of 100,000 against the rebels, who were almost all slaughtered in their fortress. Japanese Christianity was thus virtually eradicated.

The short-lived uprising fed the government's paranoia. Aside from a fear of Christianity, the government was also worried that the lords along the western coast might grow too powerful from foreign trade and form alliances with European powers. Decrees issued in

TEXT CONTINUED ON PAGE 152

PRECIOUS THINGS OF THE NŌ

Upon the simplest of stages, before the most aristocratic of audiences, Japanese actors and musicians perfected one of the truly unique forms of theater in the world, the solemn Nō drama. Nō, meaning "accomplishment," combined mime, dance, chant, music, and especially costume into an otherworldly experience that surpassed being mere entertainment to powerful military families of the sixteenth century. For after Shogun Tokugawa Ieyasu decreed it the official theater of Japan, performances of the elegant, rarefied Nō—which had actually begun in the fourteenth century—constituted great state occasions. Prominent families of the time actually studied Nō themselves and patronized it by building stages in their mansions and supporting troupes of actors. Wealthy daimyos, or nobles, even competed with one another in amassing *ontaisetsu ondōgu*, the "precious objects" of Nō, such as the robes and masks from the Tokugawa collection on these and the following pages.

Though the Nō plays tell rather simple stories—the repertoire consists almost exclusively of tales of military heroes, madwomen, demons, and gods—it does so in a highly stylized manner, relating the adventures with visual flourish and to the accompaniment of flutes and drums. Since the stage is essentially bare, the perform-

The lock of bangs bisecting the brow above identifies this Nō mask as Kasshiki, originally the name for acolytes serving in a Zen temple. Wearing the mask, an actor could portray a lay priest or a young entertainer—both somewhat effeminate. The lips, painted with red clay, are particularly lifelike.

ers' robes and masks are more like sets than costumes and are crucial to the unfolding drama. In fact the Nō actor achieves perfection in his art as much in his selection of robe and mask as by his interpretive movements.

The masks, sculpted of Japanese cypress, represent idealized personalities of both human and superhuman characters, and each has its own name. Seemingly fixed in expression, the mask comes to life when properly worn, the actor turning his head just enough to catch light and shadow, which infuses his wooden face with emotion. The actor's voice resonates through the thin mask, which has only tiny holes for eyes, ears, and mouth. Nō robes are among the supreme achievements of the textile arts, usually made of silk brocades, satins, and gauzes. Gold thread embroidery covers the intensely colored fabrics with Buddhist symbols, nature motifs, and family crests. The actor, his body lost in the bulk of his costume, displays the virtues and vices of his character in the material, weave, and decoration of his robe.

The privileged members of Tokugawa society loved the Nō, rewarding those actors and musicians who gave them pleasure—and punishing those who failed to do so. The unfortunate actor who misstepped or musician who misplayed in performance might be banished.

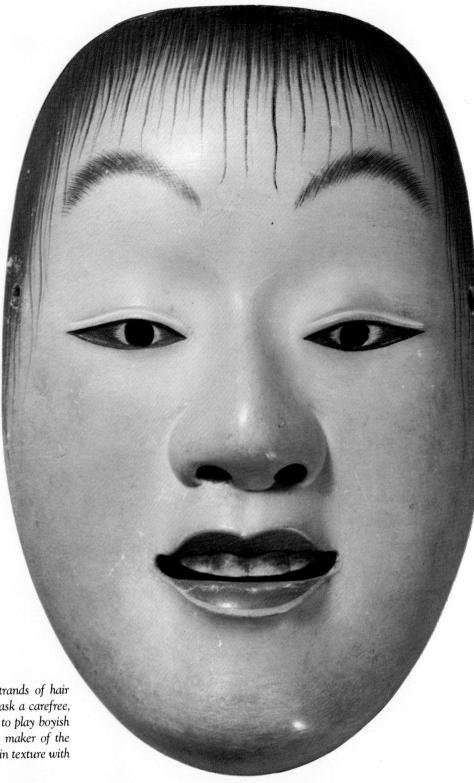

High, arched eyebrows and loose strands of hair spilling over the forehead give this mask a carefree, playful countenance. Actors wore it to play boyish characters. The seventeenth-century maker of the mask achieved remarkably realistic skin texture with the strokes of his paintbrush.

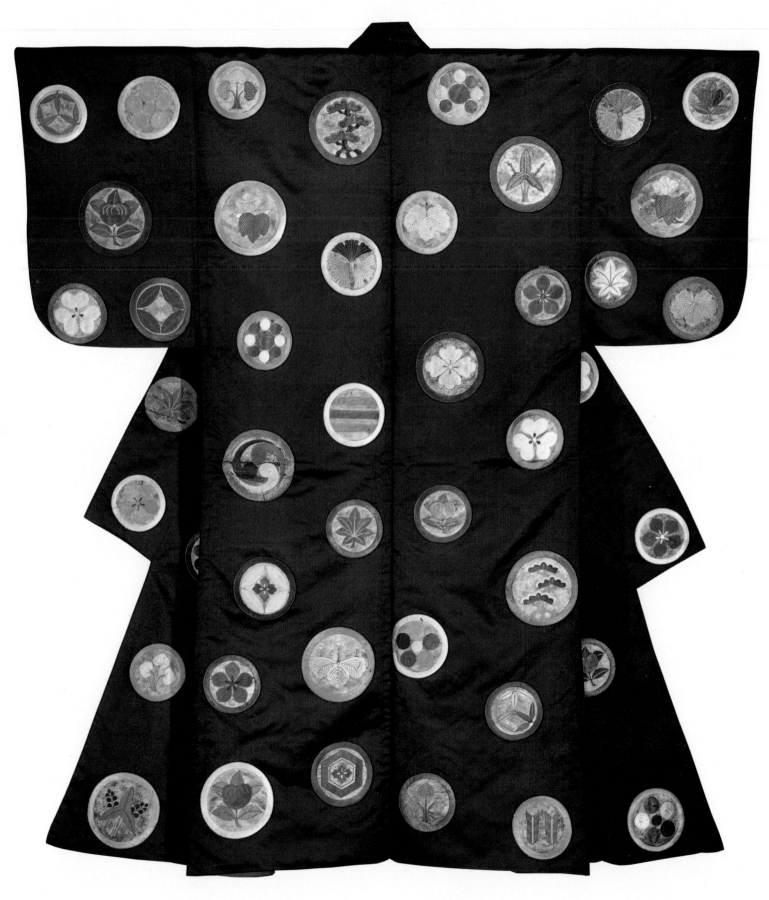

Crests of gold foil embroidered onto this deep-blue silk Nō robe represent the Tokugawa family and various plants and animals that have Buddhist meanings. In this flashy costume a Nō actor portrayed a woman possessed by demons.

Abstract designs in Nō robes, such as the zigzag above, contrasted with the more literal symbolism of other costumes in the drama. The curved shapes are based on cloud-shaped gongs used to announce meditation periods in Zen monasteries.

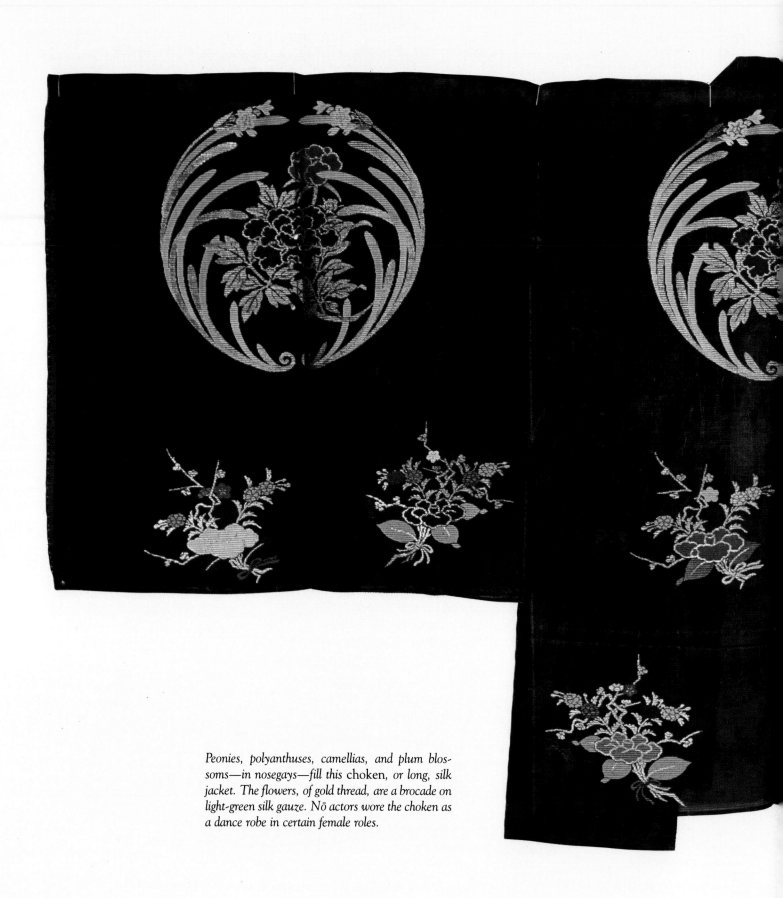

Peonies, polyanthuses, camellias, and plum blossoms—in nosegays—fill this choken, or long, silk jacket. The flowers, of gold thread, are a brocade on light-green silk gauze. Nō actors wore the choken as a dance robe in certain female roles.

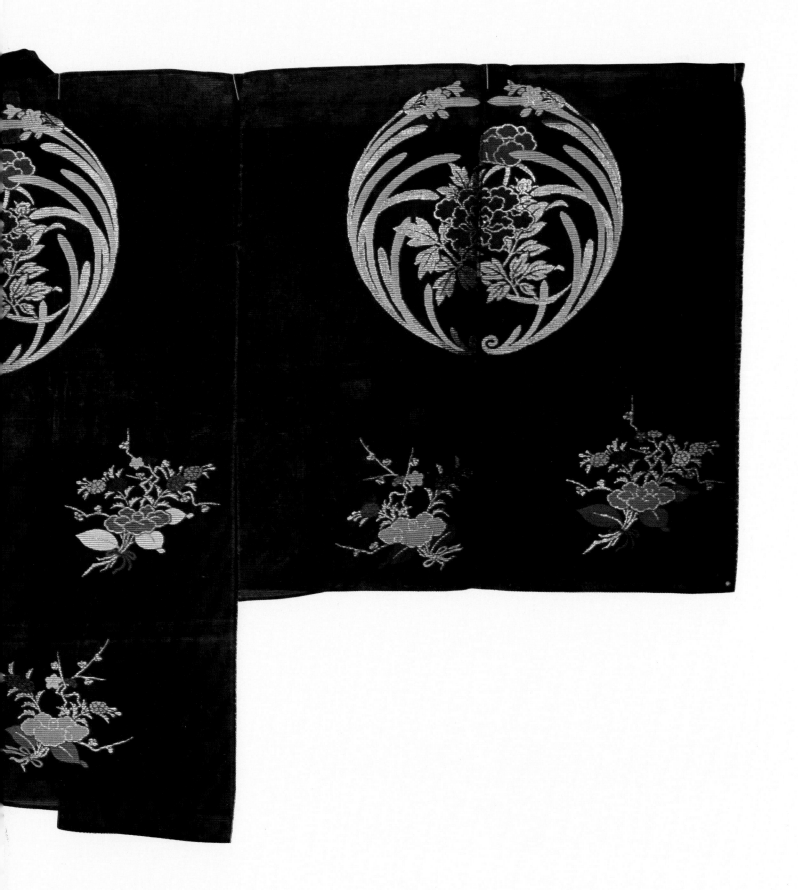

TEXT CONTINUED FROM PAGE 145

1633 and 1635, before the Christian revolt, had forbidden Japanese to leave the country and granted limited trade privileges to the Chinese, the Dutch, and the Portuguese. After the revolt the ships of Portugal, a Catholic country, were also banned. Most of the Portuguese delegation who arrived in Japan in 1640 to ask for a change of policy were beheaded. Christianity in Japan was dead. Curiously enough, by the mid-seventeenth century, the Japanese had gradually but quite as deliberately succeeded in stamping out another Western import—firearms. Adept as they were at the manufacture and use of muskets and cannons, they shut down their munitions works and returned to the sword.

The Tokugawa shoguns ruled Japan for more than two and a half centuries, bringing peace and prosperity, though at a heavy price. Despite the exclusion laws and the abrupt loss of most foreign trade, the Japanese grew richer. Townspeople in particular grew wealthy as markets sprang up around the castles of the shogunate. The merchants made fortunes transporting produce and luxury goods to these markets, which attracted the daimyos and their families. The daimyos spent heavily for luxuries—clothes for their wives, expensive lacquerware, elaborate carriages—and enriched the merchants. When their funds were exhausted, the daimyos then borrowed from their merchants, who piled up ever-greater fortunes.

The newly rich merchants of Edo provoked some social tension because merchants had always been a despised group in Japan, the lowest members of the pecking order. As long as the merchants were few and relatively unobtrusive, the shoguns tolerated them. But by the end of the seventeenth century these social misfits aroused such annoyance with their money—at a time when many of the ruling daimyos were penniless—that the Tokugawa government issued sumptuary laws to halt the unseemly parading of wealth: "Townsmen and servants should not wear silk. Townsmen should not wear cloth mantles. Townsmen should not live extravagantly. Townsmen should not give lavish entertainments."

The ban had little effect on the townspeople, who continued to do as they pleased. The theater of the non-nobility was Kabuki, a

The family of a noble sits before a lovely landscape screen playing a game, making music, and composing love letters. This seventeenth-century painting on gold leaf shows the luxurious life enjoyed by the privileged classes under the Tokugawa shogunate.

high-spirited, melodramatic, often violent stage performance, which the shoguns unwittingly spiced up when they forbade actresses from appearing in them. Actors promptly dressed up as women, affected feminine postures and speech, and acted the female roles with élan. Since many of the Kabuki plays dealt with illicit romance, the enforced use of males in female roles only enhanced the hilarity and irony. As with Nō drama, much of the appeal of Kabuki was visual: the actors wore sumptuous costumes, which the residents of Edo made into fashions, and Kabuki heightened everyone's interest in wearing the finest clothes.

Shogun Yoshimune, a descendant of Ieyasu, who ruled from 1716 to 1745, renewed the official campaign of frugality. He tried to limit the amount of gold thread in dresses, forbade the purchase of expensive lacquerware, and set down a rule for weddings: "The number of palanquins at a wedding procession shall not exceed ten."

Yoshimune was not merely a social meddler; he was genuinely worried over an economy that had suffered severely from frivolous extravagance and from a crop failure in 1732. A serious-minded ruler, he studied the books and scientific instruments that trickled in from the outside world through the Dutch traders at Nagasaki. *Rangaku,* or "Dutch learning," was the name the Japanese applied to Western technology and thought. Yoshimune asked a scholar to prepare a Japanese-Dutch dictionary to aid the flow of information, and he dispatched scholars to pump the Dutch for information on tides, eclipses, and calendars.

Yoshimune's successors were not nearly so imaginative and far-sighted as he was. The shogunate grew more conservative and suspicious of outsiders. Recurring famines, peasant unrest, and dangerously large numbers of idle soldiers thronging the cities greatly undermined the strength of the Tokugawa shogunate as it entered the nineteenth century. At this unstable moment the world that the shoguns so wanted to shut out was inexorably forcing its way in.

By the mid-nineteenth century the Pacific Ocean, once a vast, empty buffer between Japan and the rest of the world, was alive with shipping. In the typhoon-swept waters around Japan, captains

Two shy lovers—a lady of the Tokugawa family, center, and the handsome samurai general, at right—exchange letters through the go-between, at left. Another woman provides musical accompaniment in this anonymous painting from the first half of the seventeenth century.

needed safe ports for shelter. With the advent of steam power, the world's navies needed distant coaling stations. And the expanding American trade empire needed new markets.

On March 8, 1854, Commodore Matthew Calbraith Perry, who arrived with ten steam-powered American gunboats, came ashore at Kanagawa Harbor, near what is today called Tōkyō Bay. The year before, he had delivered a letter from President Millard Fillmore to the shogun's officials. The letter asked for good treatment of American soldiers shipwrecked on Japan's shores, for a coaling station, and for the opening of trade. In an unprecedented step the shogun consulted with the emperor and all the daimyos, to ask how he should reply. They resisted, objected, and temporized, but in the end the answer Perry received was the answer of the whole nation— American ships could call on Japan for coal, American sailors could find safety there, a United States consul could take up residence, and a commercial treaty would be worked out.

Beset as it was from without and within, the Tokugawa shogunate fell. The Western world, with its fluid class system, its need for world markets, and its quest for colonies, had overtaken isolationist Japan. In 1868 Emperor Meiji (his name means "enlightened government") acceded to power, and with this restoration of the ancient imperium, the modern era began.

Just before he died, in 1616, the first Tokugawa shogun, Ieyasu, had chosen his burial site: a sacred place revered as the home of spirits, in the Nikkō mountains north of Edo. He was laid to rest in a magnificent mausoleum where, he said, "My spirit will abide. . . long able to protect my country and my descendants." Shining with gold and lacquer, terrifying in its profusion of carved dragons, lions, and elephants, the shrine accompanying Ieyasu's tomb has stood as a symbol of the power and mystique both of Ieyasu and of the Tokugawa. The Nikkō shrine, the matchless Kamakura armor, the sword blades with their millions of invisible steel folds, the exquisite sutra fans of Heian-kyō, the stringed instruments of Nara, the Zen gardens are all, in their way, emblematic of the Japanese past and of the ancient sensibilities that still inform the country.

THE SUN GOD'S TEMPLE

The main hall of the Nikkō temple complex is part of the shrine of Tokugawa Ieyasu spanning a hillside. This view of rooftops is from the heights of a Japanese cedar forest.

The shogun Tokugawa Ieyasu intended his countrymen to revere him forever and toward that end ordered the construction of an awesome temple complex, the Tōshō-gū. The site he chose was a hillside near the Daiya River at Nikkō, an area of ancient mountain worship. Over fifteen thousand men—including designers, carpenters, lacquerers, and gilders—labored for twenty years, long after Ieyasu died, building the shrine to a man who considered himself a god. The plan of the Tōshō-gū at Nikkō is like that of a fortified castle, with guardhouses, concentric walls, and imposing gates that protect the inner sanctum; the architecture generally reflects a Chinese style.

The construction of the Tōshō-gū was no doubt the crowning achievement in the lives of the artists who worked on the shrine, especially in a country that ranks even its carpenters as skilled artisans. The decoration is so abundant that it hides the basic structures: columns seem less the functional supports of balconies than surfaces around which dragons coil and vines twine. Gleaming lacquer and goldwork adorn much of the basic construction.

Ieyasu died before the Tōshō-gū was completed, but in 1617, on the first anniversary of his death, a magnificent cortege—carrying out the shogun's last wishes—delivered his body to the shrine. There his subjects exalted him as the Buddha Incarnate, sun god of the East.

The Yōmei-mon, or "gate of sunlight," leads to the inner sanctum of the Tokugawa shrine. Though its size is modest—twenty-two feet wide and thirty-seven feet high—grand embellishments on the gabled gate awed visitors to Ieyasu's shrine: sculptures of fantastic birds, lions, and dragons cover the two-story structure in brilliant colors and gold. Bronze sconces provided nighttime illumination for the richly sculpted panels on the side of the building.

Golden-eyed lions carved on brackets support a veranda of the gate of sunlight (pages 156–157). The snarling, fanciful beasts are Buddhist emblems of power.

A man bestrides a bird beneath the gilded brackets supporting the roof of the magnificent gate of sunlight. The man and bird might suggest the skyward journey of the deified shogun Ieyasu.

The Kara-mon, a Chinese-style gate, of the Tōshō-
gū provides access through the sacred wall toward the
shrine of Tokugawa Ieyasu. The doorway and its
frieze are alive with human and beastly figures, and
serpents coil around the columns. Two great, bronze
dragons slither across the tile roof of the gate.

Graceful birds, probably cranes, swoop beneath a lattice panel in this section of the lacquered, painted, and gilded wall enclosing the main compound of the Tōshō-gū. The birds are an appropriate embellishment for the shrine of a man who desired immortality as much as Ieyasu did: according to Japanese belief the crane represents a thousand years of life.

OVERLEAF: *Stylized waves, gentle in appearance but great in their power, envelop the wall of the Kara-mon gate. Sculpted of wood and gilded, these waves might symbolize the masterful strategy of an ideal warrior such as Tokugawa Ieyasu, for the constant ebb and flow of the ocean embodies the essence of strong military planning.*

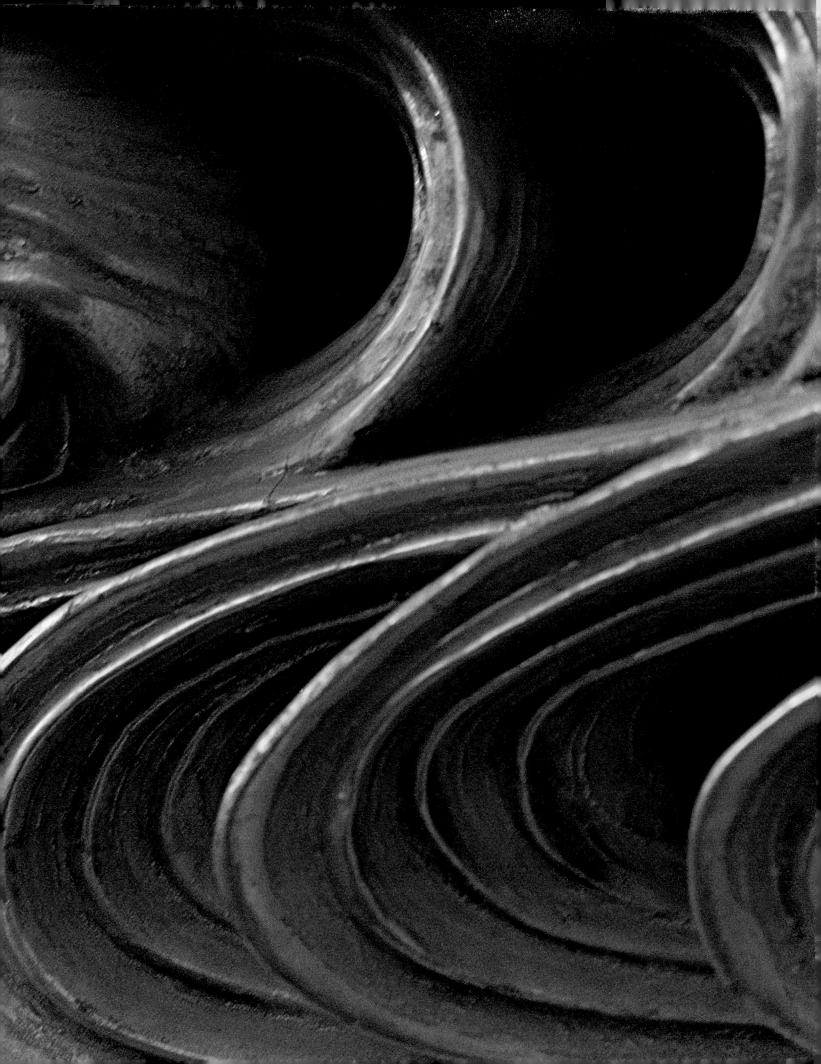

The main sanctuary, above and in detail opposite, is probably the most boldly colored and heavily embellished of the Tōshō-gū buildings. Beyond the golden doors lie the private shogunal chambers where successors of Ieyasu could meditate. The sanctuary, from its white posts laced with gold to the arabesque trim beneath the eaves, is filled with sculpted symbols, including mythical beasts.

OVERLEAF: A gold-trimmed roof crowns the main shrine of the Tōshō-gū. The sloping cylindrical tiles end in gilded medallions bearing stylized hollyhocks, the official crest of the Tokugawa family.

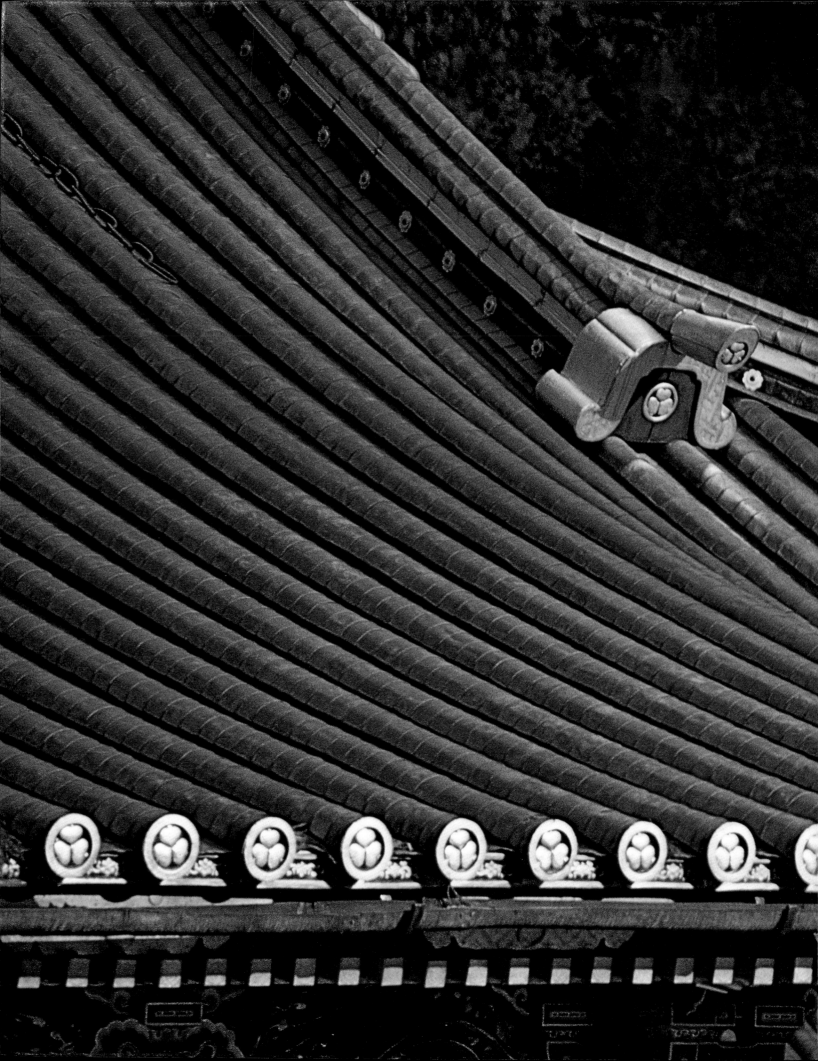

JAPAN: A CHRONOLOGY

PERIOD	PEOPLE AND EVENTS		ART AND ARCHITECTURE	
EARLY HISTORIC	c. 500	Soga family rules imperial court		
	552	Korean monks introduce Buddhism to Japan		
		Chinese civilization influences Japan		
	593–622	Prince Shōtoku is regent; firmly establishes Buddhism and emulates China		
	c. 600	Soga family toppled; Fujiwara family starts rise to power	607	Shōtoku builds Hōryū-ji temple complex to house imperial treasures
	646	Fujiwara decree land reforms		
NARA	710	Nara becomes first permanent capital		
	724	Shōmu ascends throne as emperor		
	c. 740	Buddhism becomes court religion		
	749	Empress Kōken takes throne		
			752	Shōmu dedicates temple of the Great Buddha at the Tōdai-ji
	782	Kammu becomes emperor		
	784	Kammu moves capital to Nagaoka		
HEIAN	794	Kammu founds new capital, Heian-kyō, on site of present-day Kyōto		
	805	Kammu dies		
	r. 889–897	Emperor Uda		
			c. 900	Calligraphy and poetry are important aspects of Heian court life
			c. 950	Women use kana, or syllabic writing, in poems, diaries, and novels
	r. 985–986	Emperor Kazan		
	r. 986–1011	Emperor Ichijō		
	995–1028	Fujiwara Michinaga rules behind the throne	c. 1003	Sei Shōnagon writes The Pillow Book and Lady Murasaki writes Tale of Genji
	r. 1012–1016	Emperor Sanjō		
			1022	Michinaga dedicates the temple of Hōjō-ji in Kyōto
	c. 1150	The Minamoto and Taira clans dominate the emperor		
	r. 1156–1158	Emperor Go-Shirakawa		
	1160	Minamoto and Taira battle; Taira leader Kiyomori takes control of central government		
	1180–1185	Gempei War—epic battles between Minamoto and Taira		
	1181	Kiyomori dies; Yoritomo, leader of Minamoto, begins to set up his Bakufu government at Kamakura		
	r. 1181–1183	Emperor Antoku		
KAMAKURA	r. 1184–1198	Emperor Go-Toba		
	1185	Battle of Danno-ura; Minamoto crush Taira, making Yoritomo overlord of Japan		
			c. 1190	The art of making swords and armor reaches height
	1192	Go-Toba names Yoritomo shogun; Kamakura becomes military capital		
	1268	Kublai Khan sends ambassadors to Japan demanding submission to the Mongols		

PERIOD	PEOPLE AND EVENTS		ART AND ARCHITECTURE	
KAMAKURA (continued)	1274, 1281	Mongols attack Japan and are repelled by the samurai		
	r. 1319–1338	Emperor Go-Daigo		
	1336	Ashikaga Takauji captures Kyōto and sets up puppet court there; Go-Daigo flees south and establishes rival court		
MUROMACHI	1338	Takauji becomes shogun, but rival courts continue to fight	c. 1340	Ashikaga build palaces in Muromachi quarter of Kyōto
	1367	Ashikaga Yoshimitsu becomes shogun	14th–16th c.	Zen Buddhism influences architecture and painting Garden landscaping in Kyōto reaches its peak
			1397	Golden Pavilion built for Yoshimitsu's retirement
	r. 1429–1465	Emperor Go-Hanazono		
	1449	Yoshimasa succeeds to shogunate		
	c. 1450	Yoshimasa develops Zen ritual of tea drinking ceremony		
	1467	Onin War breaks out, causing collapse of shogunate	c. 1483	Yoshimasa builds Silver Pavilion estate outside Kyōto
	1490–1600	Period of the Warring States		
	1542	First Europeans land in Japan, at Tanegashima, bringing muskets	c. 1550	Master potter Chōjirō founds raku pottery, used especially for tea ceremonies
	1560	Oda Nobunaga, great military commander, wins his first battle		
	1568	Nobunaga enters Kyōto and becomes deputy shogun		
	1582	Nobunaga is assassinated and Toyotomi Hideyoshi, a high-ranking officer, is recognized as new leader	1583	Work on Osaka Castle begins
			c. 1590	Hasegawa Tōhaku paints screens for Hideyoshi
	1592	Hideyoshi rules a united Japan Hideyoshi launches invasion of Korea, but ultimately withdraws		
	1598	Tokugawa Ieyasu succeeds Hideyoshi		
TOKUGAWA	1603	Ieyasu becomes shogun; establishes capital at Edo (today Tōkyō)		
	c. 1604	Ieyasu forms "nobility town," where he sends emperor and nobles	c. 1604	Ieyasu decrees Nō the official theater of Japan, giving rise to beautiful robes and masks
	1605	Ieyasu's son, Hidetada, succeeds as shogun		
	1614	Ieyasu besieges Toyotomi Hideyori at Osaka Castle; confrontation ends in Hideyori's suicide, leaving Ieyasu undisputed master of Japan Edict bans Christianity	1616	Ieyasu chooses his burial site at Nikkō, where Tōshō-gū temple complex is built
	1635	Trade greatly restricted		
	1637	Christian revolt	c. 1640	Kabuki, the theater of the non-nobility, flourishes in Edo
	1716	Tokugawa Yoshimune succeeds as shogun		
	1854	Commodore Perry arrives in Japan from United States, beginning era of trade		
	1868	Emperor Meiji accedes to power		

ACKNOWLEDGMENTS & CREDITS

Abbreviations:
CI—Chishaku-in, Kyōto
STH—Shōsō-in Treasure House, Nara

TRF—Tokugawa Reimeikai Foundation, Tōkyō
TNM—Tōkyō National Museum

We would like to thank the following for their assistance: Dr. Walter A. Compton, Elkhart, Indiana; Deanna Cross and Franklin Riehlman, Photographic Services, The Metropolitan Museum of Art, N.Y.; Laveta Emery, Photographic Services, Freer Gallery of Art, Washington, D.C.; Peter M. Grilli, Film Center & Education, Japan Society, Inc., N.Y.; Seizo Hayashiya, Applied Arts Department, TNM; Shizuo Imaizumi, New York Ki Society; Tak Inagaki, N.Y.; Masahiko Kawahara, Applied Arts Department, Kyōto National Museum; Rt. Rev. Jōsen Kenchu, Hōryū-ji, Nara; Shigemi Komatsu, Fine Arts Department, TNM; Martin Lorber, Sotheby Parke Bernet, Inc., N.Y.; Julia Meech-Pekarik, Department of Far Eastern Art, The Metropolitan Museum of Art, N.Y.; Masako Miyahara, Ronald Louis Nado, and Hisashi Yamada, Urasenke Tea Ceremony Society, N.Y.; Doris Mullane, Daiichi Seihan (USA) Inc., N.Y.; Kenji Numata, Society for Preservation of Japanese Art Swords; Sachiro Nanami and Masakatsu Wajima, Japan Information Center, N.Y.; Dr. Helmut Nickel and Morihiro Ogawa, Department of Arms & Armor, The Metropolitan Museum of Art, N.Y.; Margo Paul, N.Y.; Andrew Pekarik, Mary and Jackson Burke Collection, N.Y.; Hiroaki Sato, N.Y.; Pat Sherman, Photographic Services, Museum of Fine Arts, Boston; Yoshinobu Tokugawa, TRF; Noboru Yokota, Daiichi Seihan Co. Ltd., Tōkyō; Frank T. Yorichika, East Asian Library, Columbia University, N.Y.

Maps by H. Shaw Borst
Endsheet design by Cockerell Bindery/TALAS

Cover: Metropolitan Museum of Art, N.Y. 2: Museum of Fine Arts, Boston. 4–5: TNM. 6: Asuka-En, Inc.; Hōryū-ji, Nara. 10: Tōdai-ji, Nara. 12: TNM. 13: Bradley Smith/Gemini Smith Inc. 14–15: Asuka-En, Inc.; Hōryū-ji, Nara. 16–17: STH. 18: Yakushi-ji, Nara. 19–31: SHT. 32–33: Bradley Smith/Gemini Smith Inc. 34: Ise Shrine, Mie. 35: Gotō Art Museum, Tōkyō. 37: Freer Gallery of Art, Washington, D.C. 38–39: Fujita Art Museum, Osaka. 40–41: TRF. 42: Itsukushima Shrine, Hiroshima. 43: Fujita Art Museum, Osaka. 44: Yamato Bunkakun, Nara. 46–47: Gotō Art Museum, Tōkyō. 48–53: Shitennō-ji, Osaka. 54–55: O.E. Nelson, Mary and Jackson Burke Collection, N.Y. 56–57: TNM. 58–59: Imperial Household Collection. 60–61: Bradley Smith/Gemini Smith Inc. 62–63: Kita-in, Saitama Prefecture. 64–65: Otsuka Kogeisha Inc.; Private Collection. 66–67: Imperial Household Collection. 68–69 (bottom): Otsuka Kogeisha Inc.; Shirayama Hime Shrine, Ishikawa. 68–69 (top): TRF. 70: Holland Press, London. 71: Metropolitan Museum of Art, N.Y. 72: Kita-in, Saitama Prefecture. 73: Museum of Fine Arts, Boston. 74–75: Itsukushima Shrine, Hiroshima. 76: Oyamazumi Shrine, Ehime. 77: Itsukushima Shrine, Hiroshima. 78: Oyamazumi Shrine, Ehime. 79: Yoshimizu Shrine, Nara. 80: Eisei Bunko Library, Tōkyō. 81: Kasuga Taisha, Nara. 82–83: Kushibiki Hachiman-gū, Aomori. 84–85: Shogakukan Publishing Co.; Kushibiki Hachiman-gū, Aomori. 86–87: TNM. 88–89: Bradley Smith/Gemini Smith Inc. 90: Hatakeyama Art Museum, Tōkyō. 91: Kogaku-ji, Yamanashi Prefecture. 92–93: Myōshin-ji, Kyōto. 94: Nanzen-ji, Kyōto. 95: Shostal Associates, Inc. 96-109: Takeji Iwamiya/Pacific Press Service, Tōkyō. 110–111: Itsuo Art Museum, Osaka. 112–113: Hosomi Collection, Osaka. 114–115: Kyōto National Museum. 116–117: Kodai-ji, Kyōto. 118 (top): Kitamura Museum, Kyōto. 118–119: Nezu Art Museum, Tōkyō. 119 (top): TNM. 119 (center): Private Collection. 119 (bottom): Urasenke Foundation, Kyōto. 120 (top): Saga Collection, Ishiwara Prefecture. 120 (center): Setsuzo Hinohara. 120 (bottom): Private Collection. 121 (top): Egawa Museum of Art, Hyōgo. 121 (center): Sumitomo Bank, Osaka. 121 (bottom): TNM. 122–123: Uesugi Collection, Yamagata. 124: Kyōto National Museum. 125: Shogakukan Publishing Co.; CI. 126–139: CI. 140: TRF. 142–143: Osaka-jō Castle, Osaka. 144–145: Kobe Municipal Museum of Namban Art, Hyōgo. 146–151: TRF. 152–153: Ii Collection, Shiga. 154: TRF. 155: Marc Riboud, Paris. 156–157: Ryuji Yamazaki/Sekai Bunka Photo. 158–165: Marc Riboud, Paris. 166–167: Gakken Publishing Co. 168–169: Marc Riboud, Paris.

SUGGESTED READINGS

Elison, George and Cardwell L. Smith, *Warlords, Artists, and Commoners.* The University Press of Hawaii, 1981.

Frédéric, Louis, *Japan: Art and Civilization.* Thames and Hudson Ltd., 1971.

Hall, John Whitney, *Japan From Prehistory to Modern Times.* Dell Publishing Co., Inc., 1974.

Latourette, Kenneth Scott, *The History of Japan.* Macmillan Publishing Co., Inc., 1964.

———, *A Short History of the Far East.* Macmillan Publishing Co., Inc., 1964.

Morris, Ivan, *The World of the Shining Prince.* Penguin Books, Inc., 1979.

Morton, W. Scott, *Japan: Its History and Culture.* Thomas Y. Crowell, 1970.

Munsterberg, Hugo, *The Arts of Japan: An Illustrated History.* Charles Tuttle Co., 1978.

Sansom, George, *Japan: A Short Cultural History.* Stanford University Press, 1978.

Turnbull, S. R., *The Samurai: A Military History.* Macmillan Publishing Co., Inc., 1979.

INDEX

Page numbers in **boldface type** refer to illustrations and captions.

Printed and bound by Brepols S.A. — Turnhout, Belgium